UNCHAINED

Spiritually Smart Ways to Eliminate Anxiety,
Find Peace, and Live Free for God

ZACH RIBBLE

Copyright © 2020 by Zach Ribble.

Unchained—Spiritually Smart Ways to Eliminate Anxiety, Find Peace, and Live Free for God

All rights reserved. No part of this publication may be reproduced, distributed, or transmitted in any form or by any means, including photocopying, recording, or other electronic or mechanical methods, without the prior written permission of the publisher, except in the case of brief quotations embodied in critical reviews and certain other noncommercial uses permitted by copyright law.

Although the author and publisher have made every effort to ensure that the information in this book was correct at press time, the author and publisher do not assume and hereby disclaim any liability to any party for any loss, damage, or disruption caused by errors or omissions, whether such errors or omissions result from negligence, accident, or any other cause.

Adherence to all applicable laws and regulations, including international, federal, state and local governing professional licensing, business practices, advertising, and all other aspects of doing business in the US, Canada, or any other jurisdiction is the sole responsibility of the reader and consumer.

Neither the author nor the publisher assumes any responsibility or liability whatsoever on behalf of the consumer or reader of this material. Any perceived slight of any individual or organization is purely unintentional.

The resources in this book are provided for informational purposes only and should not be used to replace the specialized training and professional judgement of a health care or mental health care professional.

Neither the author nor the publisher can be held responsible for the use of the information provided within this book. Please always consult a trained professional before making any decision regarding treatment of yourself or others.

Scriptures taken from the Holy Bible, New International Version®, NIV®. Copyright © 1973, 1978, 1984, 2011 by Biblica, Inc.™ Used by permission of Zondervan. All rights reserved worldwide. www.zondervan.com The "NIV" and "New International Version" are trademarks registered in the United States Patent and Trademark Office by Biblica, Inc.™

Scripture quotations marked MSG are taken from THE MESSAGE, copyright © 1993, 2002, 2018 by Eugene H. Peterson. Used by permission of NavPress. All rights reserved. Represented by Tyndale House Publishers, a Division of Tyndale House Ministries.

Scripture quotations marked ESV are from the ESV® Bible (The Holy Bible, English Standard Version®), copyright © 2001 by Crossway, a publishing ministry of Good News Publishers. Used by permission. All rights reserved.

Editing by Beacon Point LLC
Cover Design by 100Covers.com
Interior Design by FormattedBooks.com

ISBN: 978-0-578-66962-5

FREE GIFT

Thank you very much for purchasing *Unchained: Spiritually Smart Ways to Eliminate Anxiety, Find Peace, and Live Free for God*. I pray this book can be a blessing to you or any friend or family member who may be going through anxiety, depression, OCD, or suffering in any way. In addition, I pray you develop a relationship with God, or continue to grow your relationship.

As a token of my appreciation, I invite you to download a free gift on my website at www.unchained-book.com/freegift. After you subscribe, you will receive a free gift with a document giving special biblical verses which have made a significant difference in my life. With the application and reflection of these verses, I believe they can help set you free from anxiety based on God's Word. You may unsubscribe from the email list at any time. We respect your privacy, and your email address will remain confidential and never shared with any third parties.

DEDICATION

I dedicate this book foremost to my beautiful wife, Jennifer Ribble. Without her challenging me, my life would not have changed in the ways it did. She gave me the little nudge we all need in life: a spark to pursue a loving relationship with our great almighty God and his son, Jesus Christ.

This story is also dedicated to my wonderful family. Lexi and Zoe, I love seeing how much you grow every day and the joy you bring to both your mom and me. To my mom and dad, Barb and Bob, you are the most amazing parents someone could ask for. To my sister, Allison, who is such a kind and amazing sister to me and aunt to my little girls. And to my in-laws, Les and Jamie, who are so caring and a hoot to be with.

Last, but not least, I dedicate this book to Pastor Luke Bedtelyon as a thank you for his spiritual guidance in this story.

*Come to me, all you who are weary and
burdened, and I will give you rest.*

*Take my yoke upon you and learn from me, for I am gentle
and humble in heart, and you will find rest for your souls.*

— MATTHEW 11:28–29

TABLE OF CONTENTS

Introduction XI

Chapter 1 — Focus 1

Chapter 2 — Forgive.............................. 13

Chapter 3 — Freedom 24

Chapter 4 — Vulnerability........................ 33

Chapter 5 — Gratitude........................... 42

Chapter 6 — Fresh 49

Chapter 7 — Humility 58

Chapter 8 — Truth 68

Chapter 9 — Gentle 77

Chapter 10 — Trust............................... 82

Chapter 11 — Fire................................ 89

About The Author 97

INTRODUCTION

Disclaimer: The details listed in this book do not come from a licensed medical professional. Also, they don't come from an ordained minister. Always seek medical assistance from a licensed doctor or mental health professional. Call 911 if you are in an emergency. Should you have spiritual questions, please reach out to an ordained minister.

With all this said, I am an average person. Let me make this very clear: I am just like anyone else. Why? I am a person who has mightily sinned, struggled, and felt emptiness. I have felt sadness, anger, jealousy, inadequacy, anxiety, and depression.

This anxiety and depression chained me down for as long as I can remember, making me feel virtually hopeless at times. The two dominated my adult life until I changed my mindset recently. Even to this day, I still feel these emotions on occasion. But the difference came with the decision to follow Jesus Christ. I've always been a believer, like many of you, but I lacked a pure application of his Word. Without the application, I was doing exactly what Satan wanted. I was falling into his trap time and time again, allowing him to take control of my life. It was all done subconsciously. Essentially, Satan was living rent-free in my head and chaining me down with a prison-like mindset.

We are in spiritual warfare. It's a battle that rages on and on throughout all our lives. From my experience, it's because Satan specializes in *lies*. This deception caused me so much mental pain and suffering throughout my life, as it has for many. Why did I fall victim to these lies? It's because I was swayed by the billions of lies Satan uses to attack God's children around the world.

Some may argue that lies are just one part of the devil's arsenal. True, but lies are the core problem. Here are a few examples:

1. A man murders someone who is having an affair with his girlfriend.

2. A teenager steals money from his parents for drugs.

3. A mother threatens another parent at a basketball game, not liking how another kid fouled her son.

4. A college student sleeps around with dozens of women, having unprotected sex.

All these examples may sound nothing like lies and just look like a person entangled in sin. But the root cause of the issue stems from lies:

1. A man turns away from God once he learns his girlfriend had an affair. The devil is telling him he is not good enough, and his girlfriend is turning away from him.

2. A teenager relies on drugs to survive the days, masking his insecurities but believing the lie that doing so will protect him from pain.

3. A mother does not trust in God and takes a situation in her own hands when she sees how a kid fouled her son. She believes she needs to threaten another parent to protect her baby, when in reality, God is looking out for all his children, and the hard foul may have simply been an accident.

4. The college student takes part in sleeping around because he lacked a father figure in his life. He sleeps around because he believes sexual immorality is no big deal and benefits him. This is the opposite of God's commandment of loving others and putting them first instead of self.

We all fall for the lies at times and run into situations where we need help. There is only one answer and one truth—Jesus Christ, our Savior, who died for our sins. He died for all our sins. We have to believe in him, trust in him, and rely on him. Yet many try to figure things out on their own or work hard enough to make it. We try to be perfect, but it's impossible. And all for what? We cannot *earn* our way to heaven or our salvation.

For example, I grew up in a nice home and community where my family was middle class. It was part of a wealthy community where everyone just tried to fit in. I attended the wealthier high school in town. The mascot for my high school was a doughboy. Yep, seriously. We were known as the Chargers, but the school and our rivals across town embraced making fun of the doughboy. *Dough* can be slang for money. The west side of my Midwest town was known as the wealthier side of town, and the east side of the city was the middle and lower classes.

This was an example of trying to earn it by following these ridiculous perceptions some had in our town. I'll admit this shaped who I was growing up. There were certain achievements that we felt we needed to accomplish. We were trying to keep up with the Joneses. How exhausting my irrational thoughts were to think that middle class was not good enough and that the goal was to achieve wealthy status. Being wealthy does not equate to being successful. It might be in the devil's eyes, but not for God. We have to decide *whom* we are living for. There is nothing wrong with trying to be wealthy as long as we remember to give and help those who are hurting and need assistance. Money should not be the motivation of our decisions or the number one desire deep down in our hearts.

This is not at all what God intended for his children. His Word says in 1 Timothy 6:10, "For the love of money is a root of all kinds of evil. Some people, eager for money, have wandered from the faith and pierced themselves with many griefs."

Biblical Lesson: The Bible states we should not grow anxious about money. We need to call upon the Lord when we are hurting financially to pay our bills and debts. In addition, becoming rich should never be our number one priority. We should not place our hope on the uncertainties of money or the stock market. Instead, we should pursue righteousness through sharing God's love, being tender-hearted to everyone, and putting our faith and hope in the Lord.

This verse from Timothy 1 6:10 does not apply to everyone in my hometown or around the world. Also, this verse doesn't mean we can't strive to be the best we can be and make good money because we all need to put food on the table. However, it becomes clear that money should never take priority over our relationship with Jesus and we can't pay our way into heaven with money.

There was something else I struggled with from my childhood. While growing up, my family was very loving. We had our share of problems like other families, but it wasn't anything substantial. One thing that was difficult for me was the fact that both my parents were teachers and I went to school in the same public-school system. Even if I didn't attend the same school or have either of my parents as a teacher, as my sister did, I still had a lot of pressure to perform and be a "good kid."

This meant that I needed to get straight *A*'s on all my report cards. While the expectation may not have been directly stated, I felt that it was implied. Of course, my parents encouraged me and expected me to perform well academically. However, they never said, "Get straight *A*'s, or you're grounded." My parents had a very positive reputation in our town, so people knew who my sister and I were. As such, I felt like I was scrutinized by everyone in the school district. Whenever I was in the public arena, I felt like a prisoner to judgement from others in school.

In Galatians 2:15–16, it says, "We who are Jews by birth and not sinful Gentiles know that a person is not justified by the works of the law, but by faith in Jesus Christ. So we, too, have put our faith in Christ Jesus that we may be justified by faith in Christ and not by the works of the law, because by the works of the law no one will be justified."

Biblical Lesson: We are justified through faith in Jesus. No good works can save us because we are all sinners, and we should not look to the law to save us. This verse should bring peace to so many of us who struggle with finding acceptance, feeling like we're good enough, finding healing, and so much more. There is freedom in Christ if we believe. Imagine if we could *live* like we were free, like our heavenly Father intended for all his children.

This is where I feel that I have grown tremendously in my walk with Christ, and I pray that everyone can experience this spiritual breakthrough. It's one thing to believe and have faith in God; it's another level when we can live free. I wish I could have recognized that I had a prison-like mindset. It took a long time for this to happen.

What I have experienced is just one story of how you can turn to God for all the issues you face. My story can help others with depression, anxiety, or who are struggling to find freedom in Christ. Everyone has a valuable story to share. God made us all unique with our own stories. We all have our personal stories of redemption because we have all sinned and we are all tarnished.

Never give up. Your story, too, is in the process of redemption. All glory goes to Jesus, who is the one hope we can always count on.

Remember: This is just the start, and you have to begin where you are to eliminate a prison-like mindset. It starts with faith in Jesus Christ, not with works or performance or by trying to impress people. You were designed to live for Christ.

Lies and deception create a plethora of issues for God's children. We all want to unchain ourselves from these lies that handicap our lives, so we often ask where the healing begins from our prison-like mindset.

Take Action: Identify the lies! Find out the lies that are obvious and others that may be subconsciously hidden from you. Write these down so you can reflect on them, and don't hesitate to ask your close friends and family to help you identify the lies in your life to help you grow.

CHAPTER 1
FOCUS

What would a story of redemption be without a struggle? Now I can say that I live free of anxiety and depression because of Jesus, but that did not come easy. It felt like a long path that dragged on for years. I had been attempting to figure out life on my own without *applying* what Jesus taught us about living free.

It's All Right to Struggle

To reach this peace and learn God's plans for me, I had to experience much internal strife. Who likes to struggle? Not many that I know of. I was especially weak mentally and spiritually because of how much anxiety and depression chained me down in life.

When my once-promising internship didn't turn into a permanent job, I felt being unemployed without a job in my career field made me look like a failure. It brought a sense of embarrassment. At the time of my suffering, I felt judged by others. In reality, though, I was the only one who felt this way. I became very hard on myself. It just continued to spiral into a deep, dark depression.

This suffering seemed unbearable for so long. I didn't know what to do. I loved God so much but didn't know how to make a change. I was completely caught up in my own mental torture, and any suffering that I encountered made me resist even more.

One thing I wish I could have looked back on and told my younger self is that it's all right to struggle. How else can one learn and grow? The Bible talks about this suffering and discusses how there can be peace from it. In Matthew 5:10, we read, "Blessed are those who are persecuted because of righteousness, for theirs is the kingdom of heaven."

Biblical Lesson: It is noble to stand firm with God when you are suffering or being attacked. Don't give in to your enemies or fall for their bait. Sometimes we want to throw in the towel and give into our anxieties and fears. Being a Christian is often a conflict with what the world views or desires. Christians are tortured and killed all around the world. Those who are loyal to the Lord are the ones who will be saved.

While I have not been physically beaten by others, I did cause my own angst from trying to be a perfectionist and being very hard on myself. Many people are their own worst enemy from putting constant pressure and expectations on themselves that aren't necessary. Thus, we create our own hell.

Seeking Help

When one experiences years of internal turmoil, it can be extremely difficult to cope and feel like others can help. Sometimes there is a stigma in society that someone is weak if they see a counselor. This is not true at all! It takes courage to seek help, but it is the right thing to do. I saw numerous doctors, Christian counselors, and psychiatrists seeking answers. Sometimes I would get clarity or solutions that would only solve my dilemmas temporarily. It would be right back to the drawing board. It was such a vicious cycle, and it was easy to feel lonely. I felt alone because I thought no one was experiencing what I was feeling in those moments.

I have an amazing wife, kids, parents, family, and friends. They all have loved me so much and have been nothing but supportive and a huge help. But they can only do so much. Ultimately, I was the one who needed to make changes. During these times, I felt alone even though I was strongly supported by many. Back when I was unemployed, I became engaged. Deep down, I felt like a man needed a good-paying job to take care of his spouse. Never once did my fiancé, family members, or friends say that I was a failure. They had my back and were there to support me. However, I was trapped in my own struggles and couldn't see, feel, or embrace the love others showed me. This is the definition of being chained down by one's own internal strife.

It's so important to remember that Jesus will *always* be with you no matter what evil you are facing. Many Bible verses reflect on this, but a few really stick out to me. In Joshua 1:9, his Word states, "Have I not commanded you? Be strong and courageous. Do not be afraid; do not be discouraged, for the Lord your God will be with you wherever you go."

Biblical Lesson: This is very powerful because the Lord is our protector. God is our refuge, and nothing else remotely comes close. Some situations in life may present giant hurdles where we don't have all the answers. It may seem very scary when we tackle challenges alone without clarity. Instead, Jesus wants us to take a leap of faith by trusting in him. He is on our team to hold and guide our hands when we feel that no one else knows exactly how we feel.

But you need to actively seek out God and ask for his help, and sometimes you have to be brave and seek help from others. It is better to communicate and ask for help than to suffer silently. God wants you to reach out because he wants all his children to prosper. Many resources exist for those struggling with mental health. I did it, and if this applies in your situation, please reach out to anyone who can be of assistance.

Focusing on the Light

While you need help from others, you also need to help yourself maintain focus. Everything in this world is temporary. We need to maintain perspective and not waste our energy on the things that really don't matter—expectations of us, the pressure to perform, trying to fit in, being the best or most successful, or making a name for ourselves. However, this doesn't mean you shouldn't care about God's children and show your light to everyone, especially since God's most important commandments are to love God and all people. But you also need to focus on yourself and making those necessary changes.

Every story of redemption starts with making those changes. My biggest issue in the past was that I was stuck in my own struggles. Clearly, I needed to change something. While I attended church, prayed often, and tried to serve others—and these are all wonderful things that should be continued to grow God's kingdom—they didn't fix the issues plaguing me until I changed my focus on the light above instead of being so self-absorbed in misery.

In my situation, the needed change wasn't some groundbreaking concept that set me in the right direction. Additionally, the event that triggered the change wasn't pretty or something I was proud of.

For years I struggled with obsessive-compulsive disorder (OCD) paired with anxiety and depression. These nasty disorders were all brutal to deal with daily. OCD would cause me to take part in some awful habits. It would range from obsessing about money, jobs, grades, health, anxiety, and more. At one point, I was obsessing about reading the Bible every night and would worry that if I didn't, then my anxiety wouldn't get better. I took something that was a great thing, reading the Bible, and turned it into a practice that only fueled my anxiety. Finally, my wife had to get on my tail and tell me that I needed to stop worrying about myself and begin focusing on helping others instead of focusing so much on my problems.

While I may have helped others in the past, my focus was still on my own issues instead of the joy that comes from helping people, so it didn't help. It wasn't working, not because serving others isn't a great way to help get out of this depressed mindset, but because I wasn't focused on the joy.

It was a challenge but also a reminder that I had to get my act together. Yes, we had an argument, but ultimately my wife was right and made me realize I was reading the Bible as if it were a task that needed to be checked off a list. I was so worried about if I could squeeze it in each night before going to bed. While Jesus wants a relationship with every single one of us, it should never be a chore. Yet this is exactly what I was making it.

While not focusing on a relationship with God was certainly a major issue, it wasn't the sole issue. However, focusing on God sheds light on the other significant problem. That night I told myself that I needed to stop focusing on my own issues, like my wife advised me, and instead purposefully focus on helping others. It didn't matter what my up-and-down emotions felt like in tough moments. I had to truly emphasize making a difference for others in every moment, whether it was at work, at home, or out in public. Regardless of personal issues going on, I always focused on assisting others. However, I was stuck on my problems in my mind no matter what was going on.

The spotlight needed to stop being on me and instead needed to be on loving God and his children. Sometimes, the truth hurts. A weightlifter will often say, "No pain, no gain." So true! A similar truth can be found in Romans 8:6–7 (MSG), "Obsession with self in these matters is a dead end; attention to God leads us out into the open, into a spacious, free life. Focusing on the self is the opposite of focusing on God. Anyone completely absorbed in self ignores God, ends up thinking more about self than God. That person ignores who God is and what he is doing." This might be a tough pill to swallow, but it's essentially what I was doing by focusing on my struggles rather than the blessings that God has given me.

Biblical Lesson: No matter how much you have sinned in your life, take heart that you will be saved by Jesus if you believe in him with all your heart. The Holy Spirit rejuvenates us to show an undeniable love to others, and gives us a life worth living. Do not be anxious about your failures, shortcomings, and weaknesses. These things are temporary and will pass away in time just like our bodies.

Fortunately, there's better news later in this chapter. In Romans 8:10–11 (MSG), his Word says,

> "But for you who welcome him, in whom he dwells—even though you still experience all the limitations of sin—you yourself experience life on God's terms. It stands to reason, doesn't it, that if the alive-and-

> present God who raised Jesus from the dead moves into your life, he'll do the same thing in you that he did in Jesus, bringing you alive as well? When God lives and breathes in you, you are delivered from that dead life. With his Spirit living in you, your body will be as alive as Christ's!"

Later on in that chapter, the Word talks about how we shouldn't give one more cent to our own do-it-yourself life. Our lives should be led by the Holy Spirit because we are not our own. We were paid for at a price. It's essentially saying there's nothing in our lives just for ourselves and that, instead, we should eagerly be led by the Spirit and asking God, our Father, about what occurs next. Oh, man, did I ever miss that memo! It's easy for me to look back and say that I've missed the mark so many times. However, I'm very thankful to God and constantly reminded that those struggles (that made no sense at the time) were meaningful and had a purpose to draw me closer to God and away from the never-ending bouts with anxiety and depression.

I'm convinced that I needed to be reprogrammed to escape the hell I put myself through. Countless lies were the source of the seemingly forever downward spiral. By believing these lies, they became a significant focus of my life. I know Satan planted a seed in my brain, heart, and soul. It grew and grew over the years and manifested itself as anxiety and depression. The more time that passed, the deeper the seed was planted and rooted further within me. The more rooted the lies became, the worse off I became, and the harder it was to break away.

The best analogy or picture that I can think of comparing this situation to is nasty, disgusting, and pointless weeds throughout a flower garden. What is more ridiculous and annoying than weeds that continuously grow in your garden and siphon the life out of the beautiful flowers? You do your best to pull all the weeds from the soil, and then a month later, you see half of the weeds back that you thought you just eliminated.

The problem is there are deeper roots beneath the soil that you were unsuccessful at eradicating. That was the story of my life for so long, literally and figuratively. I was never the best at yard work. There are family members that can attest to that. For example, our yard had a bunch of rocks by our sidewalk and in front of our house that I thought were a huge eyesore. My goal was to take out the rocks and have an area with grass and a mulched garden. Well, it took me two to three years to accomplish. I kept starting the project each year, and then before I finished, it was winter again here in the Midwest. It was during a time when surviving the day with anxiety and depression was rocking my world. Finally, when I was in a better mental state, I was able to complete the project in a three-day period when it had taken me almost three years before that! What a distraction anxiety had been for me to cause me to take years to complete a project that literally only took several days.

Just as Christ has given us freedom by dying for our sins, he did so that we may live for *him*. I've known for a long time that Jesus died for our sins, and I believed it too, but I suppose I didn't know what to do with that. The application was missing. How could it be applied without properly focusing on God? When I realized that I should stop concentrating on what I thought my life plans entailed instead of God's plans for me, life became so much more enjoyable.

Growing up, I became stressed about many different things when it pertained to my future. One moment it would be about grades, the next it would be about college, and then it would be about athletics. As a kid, it seemed like I had to *be* the best instead of *trying* my best. There's a notorious quote this reminds me of from a comedy movie starring Will Ferrell and John C. Reilly called *Talladega Nights*. The character, a race car driver named Ricky Bobby, told everyone that "if you ain't first, you're last." It was a hilarious movie that had nonstop chuckles. This quote helped make the movie one of the most-talked-about comedies. While this saying is funny in the context of the movie, so many people live their lives this way because of how they were raised, the environment they grew up in, or a variety of other factors.

This whole concept of having to be number one becomes a lie when this takes priority over a relationship with Jesus. If someone fails to live up to such expectations, the thirst for success only continues to grow and grow. For some, like my past self, this thirst becomes an obsession that lingers. Eventually, it becomes ingrained in your brain, goes unchecked, and becomes part of your blueprint. Then it goes unnoticed and plays a major role in your beliefs, thoughts, feelings, and emotions. You are completely unaware of what is happening, and you wouldn't even realize that Satan is persuading your thinking.

Biblical Lesson: We need to recognize Jesus everyday. He must become our number one priority if he isn't already. Christ died for our sins and paid the ultimate price. We need to put ourselves out there by publicly identifying with the Lord even when there is resistance. In addition, we must focus less on earthly rewards and more on Jesus and his plans for us.

Satan does not have to be our puppet master. Why would anyone want to be strung around by the Evil One? However, Satan creates lies that we are alone, not good enough, not loved, unliked, not safe, that the world is out to get us, and that we should look out for ourselves first and foremost. If we buy into these deceptions, then we will fall. This is why it is paramount that we put God first in everything. In Matthew 10:38–39, Jesus says, "Whoever does not take up their cross and follow me is not worthy of me. Whoever finds their life will lose it, and whoever loses their life for my sake will find it."

In life, I have found myself so often upset because life didn't go the way I wanted it to go for me. Why didn't I get that job? How come I'm not getting more playing time? How will I pay the bills? Why didn't she give me an *A* on my research paper? These are all things we can care about, but to beat ourselves over it isn't what Christ intended for us. We must focus on him in our struggles and learn what his plans are for us.

Remember: Your legacy will be determined by how you lived for God and his children, not how you suffered on this earth. Your pain is only temporary, so put your focus on what is forever: God's love. It will take weeks to months or longer, but it will work and be worth it.

Take Action: Don't spend another moment caught up in your own misery. Deliberately focus on other people no matter what degree you are suffering internally. Focus your attention only on the Lord and what his will is for you.

CHAPTER 2
FORGIVE

What you focus on in your life can single-handedly make every one of your days either brighter or darker. Focusing on making an impact on others can give you a sunny outlook. If you have suffered from anxiety, depression, or any type of mental illness, then you know how severe the mental, physical, and spiritual turmoil can be on your soul.

I loathed the days when it took every ounce of my body and mind just to keep it together throughout the entire day. Some days I would do yoga, breathing exercises, meditation, and positive thinking exercises just to reduce my anxiety a little bit. As I was just hanging by a thread some days, taking on any additional stress at work or home felt like it would just put me over the top. I was never suicidal, but I was such a hot mess that, a few times, I considered getting committed to the psychiatric ward. I never actually did this, but it crossed my mind a few times. The turmoil was causing me to act and feel like I was crazy.

On hundreds and hundreds of occasions, I beat myself up over being a perfectionist, being too critical, failing, not fitting in, and feeling worthless. Have you ever done any of these things? What was it that plagued you? Did you repeat the same mistakes over and over, or was it a little bit of everything?

As a kid growing up, I felt like I lived in the shadow of my father. My dad has always been a great role model for me. He was a hero too. He received an award of recognition from President Reagan for saving many people's lives as a volunteer firefighter. In addition, my dad was a gifted teacher that many of his former students gushed to me about, and the same thing applied to him as a middle and high school coach of numerous sports. However, it was another one of his accomplishments that I really wanted to live up to.

My dad was a supremely talented basketball player in high school. It was always his success as a player that I felt I had to live up to. My parents never said that I needed to accomplish what my father did in basketball. But my dad would remind me that I needed to put in hours of practice instead of playing video games.

There's nothing wrong with that because it's simply a true statement. I knew as a kid that my dad earned a college scholarship as a basketball player, and I wanted to make my parents proud. Yet I knew that the competition in my grade was steep. One talented player happened to be the son of the longtime boys' varsity basketball coach, and I knew I would have to go the extra mile to become a better player than the coach's son. Ultimately, he was the best player in our grade, was a four-time varsity starter, and earned a college scholarship. It wasn't just the coach's son that I compared myself to but anyone else who was considered in the top-ten range.

This continuous competition and comparison among athletes were just mentally and physically grinding. I considered it somewhat of an accomplishment to make the varsity team after being called up for the playoffs as a sophomore. Once my junior season rolled around, I figured I would make the starting lineup. I was wrong. Some sophomores came up, and I moved down the bench. When I did play, I didn't play well enough. My feelings were all over the place. I was angry, disappointed, flabbergasted, hurt, and wanted to cry at times. Finally, with a few games left in my junior year, I was emotionally drained and embarrassed. Once my parents saw how upset I was, I balled my eyes out, and I just sat down on the kitchen floor, letting all my emotions out. I told them a million things that night, but I basically told them as I sobbed that I felt like a failure, I let them down, I didn't enjoy it anymore, and I didn't want to play my senior year. They were compassionate and tried telling me that I was not a failure and didn't have to do something I didn't enjoy anymore.

Forgive Yourself

Sometimes I wish I could hop in a time machine and give my younger self some practical advice. One thing would be to forgive myself for all the constant pressure I put on myself. There was no need to be perfect despite the tremendous amount of internal pressure. When I learned to forgive myself, it felt like so many pounds of unnecessary stress just melted away. I felt unchained and set free.

Jesus intended for us to forgive ourselves and not live with a heavy burden. Jesus said in Matthew 11:28–29, "Come to me, all you who are weary and burdened, and I will give you rest. Take my yoke upon you and learn from me, for I am gentle and humble in heart, and you will find rest for your souls."

Biblical Lesson: Jesus is openly requesting that we approach him with all of our pain, suffering, and troubles. There is no reason not to seek him because we are dearly loved. He is approachable for all. Accepting Jesus as our Savior can help us find peace in the Lord, and give us purpose and hope spiritually. It helps us forgive ourselves as well.

When I reflect on this powerful verse, I wonder how could someone *not* turn to Jesus in troubling times? It's an open invitation for us to accept anytime, anywhere. Who wouldn't want the peace and rest that comes with knowing and loving God?

If we can confess our sins and ask for forgiveness in prayer, then the Lord can provide a path for redemption and spiritual growth. In Isaiah 44:22, the Lord said, "I have swept away your offenses like a cloud, your sins like the morning mist. Return to me, for I have redeemed you."

Biblical Lesson: God is the only one who can redeem us and set us free from our transgressions. There are no idols that can offer this. Therefore, turn only to the Lord, confess our sins, and seek forgiveness for ourselves and our enemies.

Imagine the feeling of all your burdens, shame, guilt, weaknesses, failures, and blemishes just lifted off your shoulders. No longer will they weigh you down mentally, physically, and spiritually. Some of you may wonder when that day will ever come. Believe me, I wondered the same thing. Scripture in 2 Peter 3:9 said, "The Lord is not slow in keeping his promise, as some understand slowness. Instead he is patient with you, not wanting anyone to perish, but everyone to come to repentance."

Biblical Lesson: Everything will be done on the Lord's time. It will also be done if it is according to God's will for our lives. As humans, we can naturally grow impatient because we do not understand. Everything will occur to glorify God's name, and sometimes this might involve waiting for a long time to come to repentance. As we learn more about the Lord, he wants to give us an opportunity to seek forgiveness.

Part of getting to know our heavenly Father is accepting the truth, which is that Jesus died for our sins. Why, then, is it so hard to live freely and apply this to our lives? I feel that we get caught up in our own sins and shortcomings and can't shake them. In Psalm 103:12, his Word says, "As far as the east is from the west, so far has he removed our transgressions from us." Since God has forgiven us, who are we to not forgive ourselves?

Biblical Lesson: There is no distance that can separate us from the love of Christ. The same applies to how severe our anxiety, depression, sins, and failures may be. God's light will always outshine our darkness. We just need to show humility by openly asking the Lord for forgiveness.

This one stings for me as it deals with being prideful. My father and my wife had to remind me many times about being humble. If people can never forgive themselves, then they are setting a standard for themselves above everyone else and, most importantly, God. If we turn down the forgiveness that Jesus gave us, then we are essentially saying that we are playing by a different set of rules. We have the choice because we are free. It's really a matter of deliberately changing our mindset, challenging those negative or stubborn thoughts, and changing them gradually over time.

Everyone has their own journey in which there will be obstacles and tragedies. Many will question their identity and purpose somewhere along the way, but there is only one direct way. His Word states in Proverbs 3:5–6, "Trust in the Lord with all your heart and lean not on your own understanding; in all your ways submit to him, and he will make your paths straight."

Biblical Lesson: We need not put pressure on ourselves to figure out life when we can, instead, surrender to the Lord and confidently believe in his plan for us. When all else fails, bow down, humble yourself, and turn to the Savior.

Forgive Others

Once we learn to forgive ourselves, it sets us on the right path to forgiving others. There have been so many times I've been hurt badly by insulting comments from other people. Many times I wanted to scream back at them, curse up a storm, or fight back. Did I ever really do any of these things? Not really. See, I'm an introvert, and when I feel like I'm being attacked, usually I will just take it, absorb everything, shut up, and not do a doggone thing about it. Like many introverts, I compartmentalize and analyze these destructive digs thrown at me. Eventually, it simmers slowly and steadily, and soon it reaches a boiling point. It's at that time when our emotions hit their max capacity. Generally, these results are not pretty.

Often one of the hardest times in life is in middle school. For some, it's just a matter of surviving it. I remember when I entered sixth grade that friends changed, girls became a priority, being one of the cool kids mattered, and the brands of clothes you wore were scrutinized. It was also a time to drag other kids down so you could get a laugh from friends and gain as much popularity as one could.

Kids looked for any type of weakness they could find. Mine was pretty obvious. I have always had very light blond hair since I was a baby. It quickly became a target, and a few kids started calling me albino. What they were saying wasn't even true because albinos have red eyes and I had blue eyes. This didn't seem to matter, though. At this age, the pain was insurmountable, and I couldn't muster up the courage to stand up to the bullies. This was because I felt worthless, not good enough, and ashamed of myself.

This is not God's intention for any of his children. In Isaiah 54:4, the Lord says, "Do not be afraid; you will not be put to shame. Do not fear disgrace; you will not be humiliated. You will forget the shame of your youth and remember no more the reproach of your widowhood." There is so much Scripture that speaks to how God is with us in every moment. Another great verse is in Psalm 35:5, where his Word states, "Those who look to him are radiant; their faces are never covered with shame."

Biblical Lesson: The Lord states that we will be delivered from any shame we ever encountered if we believe in him. Any rejection we receive in this world is only temporary, and we can hold our head up high because God is always with us. Do not be afraid to suffer on God's behalf because he will be with those who stand firm until the end.

We will go through various forms of suffering in our life, and it can be easy to ask, "Why me?" Only God knows the answer, but we do know that Jesus went to the cross to die for our sins so that we may be free. We were made free to live for him and shine his light throughout the world. We must do our best to be radiant in his name when we face trials.

To this day, I still remember the individual who slandered me over twenty years ago. In fact, I had minimal contact with him after sixth grade. It makes sense that we were "just kids," but that doesn't diminish the anguish it caused me as a child. I remembered it well all throughout middle school and high school, wondering how many others felt this way about me. Once college rolled around, I didn't care anymore about that, and it didn't faze me. As a kid, I wish I could have forgiven him shortly after it happened. It would have brought me a sense of freedom and peace in my childhood. I would have gained confidence in my self-esteem, knowing that my light blond hair didn't make me a lesser person. Most importantly, it would have been a way to shine God's grace to others.

It is better to help others and do something about it instead of letting the pain linger inside us. Scripture tells us in Ephesians 4:31–32, "Get rid of all bitterness, rage and anger, brawling and slander, along with every form of malice. Be kind and compassionate to one another, forgiving each other, just as in Christ God forgave you." This is something we often forget when we are in the heat of a conflict. We are trapped in that intense moment, and typically, our first goal is to protect ourselves and be on the defensive. Instead, God advises us in 1 Timothy 6:12, "Fight the good fight of the faith. Take ahold of the eternal life to which you were called when you made your good confession in the presence of many witnesses."

Biblical Lesson: Do not hold grudges and take it to the grave. Pray for wisdom as you ask for forgiveness. Depend on God when going through heated exchanges with others. We will ultimately be remembered for how we lived for Jesus in both the good and bad times.

Lean on God's Grace

When we recognize God is always with us, it can bring a great sense of peace that won't leave our cage rattled while in the midst of a storm. In addition, despite our daily battles, we need to take comfort that the war has already been won. While we are being attacked, we need to apply God's written word to our situation. In 2 Chronicles 20:17, the Lord says, "You will not have to fight this battle. Take up your positions; stand firm and see the deliverance the Lord will give you, Judah and Jerusalem. Do not be afraid; do not be discouraged. Go out to face them tomorrow, and the Lord will be with you."

Biblical Lesson: Essentially, God is telling us that while the war has been won, we still need to stand our ground while the battle is occurring. We only need to stand still, have faith, and trust in him.

After our individual battle is done, we can reflect on God's love and grace always being here for us. If we are still feeling hurt from what others have done to us, we can remember what God said in Colossians 1:13–14, "For he has rescued us from the dominion of darkness and brought us into the kingdom of the Son he loves, in whom we have redemption, the forgiveness of sins."

Biblical Lesson: It's in this forgiveness we can find healing and freedom. No one else can lift us from our burdens and wrongdoings since we are all born sinners. There is no greater gift we could ever receive. Do not deny the love that comes from the Lord.

Remember: If you confess your sins, then God will forgive you. You need to forgive yourself too to begin healing, which involves cutting yourself some slack. Ask Jesus for wisdom, as this can be very difficult for many people.

Take Action: Identify as many people, events, and situations that *trigger* your emotional pain and turmoil. Reflect on how you can forgive your enemies, and don't hold any more anger, jealousy, or bitterness inside you. Instead, forgive and live free for Jesus.

CHAPTER 3
FREEDOM

Forgiveness is a wonderful way to let go of a whole bunch of unnecessary pain. It is liberating to forgive yourself and others. This should give one a sense of freedom, which is a gift in itself.

Yet, the greatest gift God could ever give us was his son, Jesus Christ. Perhaps the most popular biblical verse ever is John 3:16 where the Word says, "For God so loved the world that he gave his one and only Son, that whoever believes in him shall not perish but have eternal life." There is no doubt—this is the best news ever!

Biblical Lesson: God sacrificed his only child to save all of humanity for everyone who believes in him. For anyone hurting, this verse provides so much hope and inspiration. It is the key to our freedom in Christ. Apply this hope whenever you are down or lost. Believe with all your heart that this is the best news ever.

So then, why don't many Christians treat it like it's the best news ever? Why don't we recognize that Jesus was given to us to die on the cross for our sins? Why don't we apply this news so that we can live freely? One reason, we could speculate, is that we can't see our Lord and we did not live at the time of Jesus preaching to his people in Israel two thousand years ago. I'm a visual learner myself, so I understand the difficulty in knowing Jesus lived. However, the Lord says right in this verse that those who *believe* in him shall not perish.

All we need to do is believe, and we can find joy. Sometimes I wonder how much better the world and all of us would be if we could see our planet through God's eyes. To witness such a thing, I once saw a truly inspirational video where a kid recorded his brother seeing the world differently for the first time. The brother was sitting in his classroom, and the school principal gave the student a pair of color-blind glasses. After he put on the glasses, the kid began laughing and crying. Several people hugged him, and he walked around the classroom, witnessing a bright-colored book, wall paintings, and then the periodic table of elements. When he saw the periodic table and all the various colors, he was stunned. The kid continued to just smile and cry at the same time since it was such an overwhelming joyous moment.

This is a small glimmer of the type of joy we can experience with our heavenly Father, except it will be infinitely times bigger! Folks who are color blind usually see what our world looks like in a limited capacity. Until they put on an expensive pair of color-blind glasses, they haven't fully seen how beautiful the world can be. When I suffered deeply from anxiety, depression, and OCD, I viewed the world as a dark place. My optics were in bad shape. Over the past few years, after I changed my focus, the beautiful light and colors became more visible. Now I view the world very differently.

Let's not kid ourselves, though. The world is a broken place. Every single one of us is imperfect in our own unique ways. Some may feel any combination of guilt, betrayal, inadequacy, shame, embarrassment, negativity, depression, jealousy, angst, and many other emotions. To all who are suffering, believe it or not, there is a purpose, and God has big plans for you to glorify him. Scripture says in Jeremiah 29:11, "'For I know the plans I have for you,' declares the Lord, 'plans to prosper you and not to harm you, plans to give you hope and a future.'"

Biblical Lesson: God is the ultimate leader for us to follow. We will have far more spiritual freedom when we wholly trust in the Lord's plans for us. This includes when we hit bumps and setbacks along the way. We will enjoy the ride a lot more and embrace our freedom when we allow our life to unfold by waiting patiently for the Lord.

Chained Down with No Freedom

Most of my life I didn't have this mentality, and I paid the price by putting myself through misery. Chained down with that prison-like mindset, I obsessed over ideas, items, and feelings that stemmed from deep-rooted lies from the devil. For months, I had an obsession with money. When my wife told me that she wanted to go back to school for dual master's and doctoral degrees in chemistry, I basically freaked out. With my wife quitting her job, I thought we might not be able to pay all our bills, student loans, and mortgage. The thought of foreclosing on our house terrified me.

It wasn't just one night that I stressed out about not having enough money to pay the bills. It was every day. The lies consumed me and stressed me out to the point where I couldn't even sleep. In fact, it wasn't uncommon for me to go back-to-back nights without sleeping. On the few nights I did sleep, it wasn't more than two or three hours—and I'm not kidding. Then, I scheduled so many appointments with a doctor, counselor, and psychiatrist. Eventually, I found a medication that was so strong it would knock me out regardless of how stressed I was.

Around the same time, another lie I was having difficulty with was feeling not good enough to accept a job promotion as a staffing manager. My supervisor believed in me and thought I would be a good fit for it. My performance had been pretty good for a long time after a rough start in the beginning. If my boss, coworkers, clients, family, and most importantly, God, believed in me and saw how successful I had been in the past, then what was the big deal? Was I the only irrational person in the equation? Without a doubt, a resounding yes. Irrational fears were festering in my soul, heart, and mind. I kept talking myself out of the opportunity.

Have you ever been presented with a great opportunity that scared you? Did you turn to Jesus and trust in him, or did you handle it alone? I definitely did the latter, turning myself into a basket case. Typically, I feel like I'm a rational person. Even while in this chaos, I knew deep down that I could handle this challenge. However, the lies won out, and I turned the promotion down because I was afraid of failure and I was too comfortable in my cushy position.

The combination of these two situations—a declined promotion opportunity and the loss of family income with my wife going back to school—made me feel like I was crazy sometimes. The web of lies became a part of who I was as a person. I continued to bury myself in a hole deeper and deeper every day. My insecurities overwhelmed me, and I selfishly became stuck in the weeds. Eventually, these deep-rooted weeds of sin became what I subconsciously worshipped. However, in my mind, I was constantly praying to God, only looking for a way to help myself. Nothing was working for years. Why didn't I ask for God's healing while also focusing on loving him and his children? It's because I was still tangled in the evil roots of the devil.

Freedom through Helping Others

Many of us have endured unbearable pain in our lives, be it from war, having been assaulted or abused, or living in violent neighborhoods. Many tragic events can cause post-traumatic stress disorder, which might last a lifetime. If there's any type of liberty we can feel, we can convert our pain and suffering to help others. See, the devil wants you to compartmentalize all that traumatic pain, let it fester, and gradually consume you. Instead, it can be used to our advantage by converting our hurt and suffering to help others. You are not alone. Others would greatly benefit from your assistance because of the trauma you've endured. In Proverbs 17:17, Scripture says, "A friend loves at all times, and a brother is born for a time of adversity."

Biblical Lesson: Christ wants us to be loyal to others at all times, especially in times of hardship and trouble. When the going gets tough, we can weed out our true friends. The Lord wants us to strive to be a good friend and lend a helping hand when times are tough. This can be a liberating feeling, especially when we have been in distress.

Don't keep your pain bottled up inside. We all have a story of redemption. Even if you feel that your trauma is too much to handle and is thus preventing you from helping others, then perhaps you need to focus on our Savior. Jesus said in Matthew 25:40, "The King will reply, 'Truly I tell you, whatever you did for one of the least of these brothers and sisters of mine, you did for me.'"

Biblical Lesson: This teaching may often be rejected in our world. Jesus said to love our enemies because they are children of God, too. It requires us to dig deep and become personally invested when caring for others. This will help unchain any fears or uncertainties we have by focusing first on serving everyone.

Finding Freedom in God

The devil is only as powerful as we make him, and there is a reason why he is beneath God, angels, and even our own two feet. However, the more lost we are, the more likely he will cause us to go off the beaten path. Scripture says in 1 Peter 5:8–10, "Be alert and of sober mind. Your enemy the devil prowls around like a roaring lion looking for someone to devour. Resist him, standing firm in the faith, because you know that the family of believers throughout the world is undergoing the same kind of suffering. And the God of all grace, who called you to his eternal glory in Christ, after you have suffered a little while, will himself restore you and make you strong, firm, and steadfast."

Biblical Lesson: When you least expect it, the devil will try to trip you up. Don't panic if something bad happens. It could potentially be a struggle that makes you stronger in the long run or might be part of God's plan. Instead, seek the Lord and a family of believers who have struggles too and can be there by your side.

God's Word is uplifting here because it's stating that any suffering we encounter can help us grow stronger in our faith and draw closer to our heavenly Father. When I severely struggled in the past, I always had faith but had a difficult time understanding the purpose and how to get out of the struggle. Sometimes I would struggle on my own, and it would just end up making things worse. If we try to fight the battle on our own, then how can we ever have freedom? We are supposed to trust God to fight our battles. In Exodus

14:14, his Word states, "The Lord will fight for you; you only need to be still."

Biblical Lesson: Life will throw us many curve balls that can be upsetting. God can intervene on our behalf if we trust in him. Do not be chained down to unfortunate events that happen in your life. They do not have to define you.

Many years I have been impatient and anxious to find out what will happen next, and with that comes a lot of wondering. Then it turns into analyzing, followed by negative thinking, and then panicking. This causes nothing good. Scripture says in Psalm 37:7–9, "Be still before the Lord and wait patiently for him; do not fret when people succeed in their ways, when they carry out their wicked schemes. Refrain from anger and turn from wrath; do not fret—it leads only to evil. For those who are evil will be destroyed, but those who hope in the Lord will inherit the land." It took years for me to heal completely. It didn't happen overnight, and it required a lot of patience.

Biblical Lesson: Do not compare yourself or your situation to your sister, best friend, neighbor, nor anyone for that matter. It will instantly steal your joy and cause stress. We may have no idea what God's will is for our lives. All we can do is pray for guidance for the Lord and patiently wait while life unfolds.

The moment you feel you are struggling, take a moment to reflect and determine the specific problem. Next, recognize that the Lord is *infinitely* bigger than your problem and believe in him with all your heart. Take the spotlight off your fear, and focus on what you are grateful for—family, friends, accomplishments, and more. If we put the attention on our issues, then this pain will only grow. Put your focus on God, and allow him to move in your life. While this is happening, remember that your pain is only temporary. It will disappear in time. See your temporary pain just like it is smoke from a fire because, ultimately, it will soon blow away. The Lord lives forever and is everlasting, so love him and his children.

God is faithful, and he will deliver you from your suffering. It is never too late. His passage in Isaiah 43:19 delivers amazing hope when he says, "See, I am doing a new thing! Now it springs up; do you not perceive it? I am making a way in the wilderness and streams in the wasteland."

Biblical Lesson: You can start healing when you believe with all your heart that God is your heavenly Father and Savior. In addition, you must focus on loving others more than your present sufferings. It's a journey of faith, and we should trust in God in each step along the way. This will give us a true sense of peace and freedom.

Remember: Change your optics. See your life through the eyes of the Lord and not through your eyes in which you suffer.

Take Action: You will experience true freedom when your life is built on the foundation of the best news ever, which is that Christ died for our sins. Help and serve others in Christ's name, but don't fall in bondage to other people by letting them stress you out.

CHAPTER 4
VULNERABILITY

Many years I felt some freedom from helping out other people, but it wasn't as much as I could have experienced. Serving others has always brought a smile to my face. Ever since I volunteered for kids in Sunday school during my high school years, it has been a privilege to help others. Those times were brief moments of hope in what I deemed a dark world, one in which I tried just to survive and protect myself. I may have shown heart at times, but it was only the slightest fraction of true love one can show others. It's a love of untapped potential that has been buried with fear.

God wants us to care for his children without being scared or being distracted by our own personal concerns. In 1 John 4:18, God says, "There is no fear in love. But perfect love drives out fear, because fear has to do with punishment. The one who fears is not made perfect in love." I long for the biggest heart that doesn't cave in to fear, which kept me trapped in my own prison of misery.

Biblical Lesson: The devil knows our weak points, so he will do anything to make us dread punishment. Instead, we need to change our view by using these scary occasions as moments of opportunity to glorify Christ. Try to view the situation as something needing God's perfect love, and see how you can be led by the Holy Spirit. Otherwise, our fear will remain in our mindset.

To combat this fear and heal, we need to be vulnerable for Jesus Christ, just as he is for everyone. Most know how he was nailed to the cross. We know the reason why, but perhaps we don't know all the details because it hurts. Perhaps reading about the crucifixion in the Bible or watching a graphic scene of it makes people uncomfortable, angry, or upset. Don't avoid it for these reasons. How will we truly understand the full impact of Jesus's ultimate sacrifice if we don't see it ourselves?

All we need to do is absorb the cost that Jesus paid for by dying for all sins. Jesus already won the war. That is perfect love. The least we can do is appreciate the ultimate sacrifice he made, witness it, take it in, reflect, and refine our lives on how we can live for him.

What It Means to Be Vulnerable

What is true vulnerability? It's more than putting yourself out there. Another level is reached when you pour all your love out and put it all on the line when everything's at stake in threatening environments. This is exactly what Jesus Christ sacrificed when he faced crucifixion.

To show an unparalleled love, we must witness and not turn an eye to the brutal beating that Christ took for every single one of us. First of all, imagine being betrayed by one of your closest friends and allies, like Jesus was with his trusted disciple, Judas Iscariot. Afterward, what would you do if soldiers and an entire crowd made a mockery of you by spitting on you and placing a crown of thorns piercing your skull? Our Savior just endured. Then imagine being punched, whipped, and then carrying a cross by yourself several times your weight. Next, one cannot fathom nails being driven into our hands and feet. Only Jesus can take all that pain away from us. Finally, watch with tears of sorrow as your Savior hangs from a cross for three hours and cries out to the Father to ask why he has been forsaken.

Reading about the crucifixion, speaking about it, hearing the story, and even writing about it truly shakes your soul. It hurts on a personal level. No matter how much it pierces our soul, we can take heart that Jesus died for our sins, overcame death, and was resurrected on Easter. Will we accept Jesus as our Savior and recognize how vulnerable and loving he was to go to the cross? Once we accept that, will we live for God and be vulnerable for him?

How to Be Vulnerable

This is no easy task by any means. I don't even think I recognized this void in my heart until the last few years, after self-reflection and praying to God. One day I let my pride get in the way. My wife and I have always done a great job raising our two little girls. We are not perfect, though, so we don't have to live our lives based on others' expectations to maintain a perfect face for society. I got upset that she accidentally cursed in front of our girls. She apologized for what she did, and this should have been the end of it.

Instead, I held on to the fear that my kids might repeat the swearing in public, making the whole family look bad. At a later time, we had a serious discussion about why I was acting like I was better than her. I have sworn plenty of times, especially when I was younger. It was not at all my intention, and I didn't even realize I was doing it, but I was worried about my pride in this situation. If my kid repeats a curse word in public, it's not the end of the world. Obviously, we acknowledged the situation and tried to prevent it from happening again in the future.

I didn't need to act like I was any different or better than my wife. After I apologized to her and confessed to the Lord for acting prideful, this concept of being vulnerable just appeared when I learned I was on edge and acting guarded. Then I realized that I should step out of my comfort zone and not put so much stock in what other people think of me. I needed to be vulnerable with a purpose of love for my wife when perhaps it felt like I was judging her for swearing. I was getting caught up in the fact that our daughter could potentially curse in front of others and then people would scrutinize us as parents.

When facing a difficult decision, consider whether you take a risk in the name of love or take the easier way out that is generally safer and more convenient. The more I try to be open-minded, the easier it is to identify these circumstances as they arise. We must always keep on high alert because the devil is always looking to kill and destroy. Reminders can certainly be useful too. In fact, Paul had a thorn from the devil in his flesh as a reminder, and Scripture in 2 Corinthians 12:7–10 states,

> "Therefore, in order to keep me from becoming conceited, I was given a thorn in my flesh, a messenger of Satan, to torment me. Three times I pleaded with the Lord to take it away from me. But he said to me, 'My grace is sufficient for you, for my power is made perfect in weakness.' Therefore I will boast all the more gladly about my weaknesses, so that Christ's power may rest on me. That is why, for Christ's sake, I delight in weaknesses, in insults, in hardships, in persecutions, in difficulties. For when I am weak, then I am strong.'"

Biblical Lesson: To know Jesus is to suffer on his behalf. When we need comfort and peace, there is no one else to turn to except for Christ. The Lord can help us become a mature follower by becoming more humble and empathetic to others. As a result, we can use this as a gift to help others. Before this all starts, we have to embrace our weaknesses.

Essentially, we need to be open to criticism, attacks, slanderings, and being wounded or hurt. We can't live life in bubble wrap. It's not feasible, so why do we even bother trying to live a protected life?

Relying on Christ

Another aspect of vulnerability is relying on Christ as he wants us to do. His grace *is* enough, regardless of the challenging situations we face in this world.

Please remember that God's grace is all you need when you feel hopeless. When you lack hope, it is better to ask for help than to suffer in silence. Satan wants you to rot away in your sorrow while chained to it for all eternity. Relying on Christ doesn't mean you don't go to other sources. Christ uses others to bless us. It's helpful to see counselors, therapists, ministers, and other licensed professionals. I went to see professionals for years. It takes time, but you can get better.

Even though I have successfully overcome anxiety on a general basis over time, the key point is that it took a long time and diligence to get better. There was no easy button to hit to make all my problems disappear instantly. I still struggle with issues sometimes today, but I am leaps and bounds ahead of where I was in the past.

Being Vulnerable Enough to Love Your Enemies

One of the most challenging situations others and I face is dealing with enemies. If someone has hurt me in the past, I often feel a lot of angst when I see them again or even daily. They have made me feel angry, bitter, depressed, and irritated. Generally, I would try to avoid them at all costs. Jesus has another idea for us. The Word states in Luke 6:35–36, "But love your enemies, do good to them, and lend to them without expecting to get anything back. Then your reward will be great, and you will be children of the Most High, because he is kind to the ungrateful and wicked. Be merciful, just as your Father is merciful."

Biblical Lesson: Often the wickedest of souls are the ones in the most need of God and saving. We can't be so quick to judge, but often when we are wounded by the enemy, all we know about that person is the pain they have inflicted on us.

Some people may ask, "What if it's the worst human being ever?" It doesn't matter. In Matthew 25:40, Jesus said, "The King will reply, 'Truly I tell you, whatever you did for one of the least of these brothers and sisters of mine, you did for me.'" This is a tough pill to swallow for some, and a few of you might even close the book now. The reason why this is such a difficult concept is that it's completely unfamiliar. Scripture states in John 18:36, "Jesus said, 'My kingdom is not of this world. If it were, my servants would fight to prevent my arrest by the Jewish leaders. But now my kingdom is from another place.'"

Not only is Jesus's kingdom not of this world, but neither are we. In John 15:18–19, Jesus said, "If the world hates you, keep in mind that it hated me first. If you belonged to the world, it would love you as its own. As it is, you do not belong to the world, but I have chosen you out of the world. This is why the world hates you."

Biblical Lesson: Jesus went to the cross to save our souls and keep us from perishing. This concept of sacrificing for others is commonly rejected by many. We have to decide if we will publicly praise the Lord and help others in his name, or if we will reject him and live by what the world tells us to do. You may be hated for following God.

Speaking of hate, too often in today's age, it's easy to get caught up in the division in our nation, and it just breaks my heart to see what is happening. We all bleed the same, so why can't we all treat each other with love and kindness? Before the political climate in our country became incredibly heated, two of my close friends in college would often argue with me about picking a side. One guy was an extremely conservative Republican, and the other was a very liberal Democrat. They enjoyed their squabbling often and typically needed a third party to settle their debate to find out who was the winner. Well, when I didn't partake, they would both turn the tables on me by making fun of me and throwing insults. Back in the day, this was one of the few times where I did the right thing by not falling into their trap.

I would ask anyone why we have to pick a side and be identified and clumped in with a certain group of people, whether it's politics, sports, businesses, or neighborhoods. There is only one answer, and that is following the Lord. In Matthew 10:37–39, Jesus said, "Anyone who loves their father or mother more than me is not worthy of me; anyone who loves their son or daughter more than me is not worthy of me. Whoever does not take up their cross and follow me is not worthy of me. Whoever finds their life will lose it, and whoever loses their life for my sake will find it."

Biblical Lesson: Losing our life to Christ is exactly how we become vulnerable for him. Will you stand up for what's right? It is exactly how we become free and live free with the Lord.

Remember: If you are a believer, reflect deep down in your soul on what it means to put yourself out there. Ask how you can pour out all your heart regardless of how uncomfortable it may be with the enemy prowling or in perilous environments.

Take Action: Humble yourself and be vulnerable for Christ. Don't be afraid by staying wrapped in bubble wrap; instead, trust in God, and get ready to become wounded to slander, attacks, and criticism, and depend humbly on the grace of the Lord.

CHAPTER 5
GRATITUDE

Being vulnerable can be quite an emotional change for many of us. Once we've learned to put ourselves out there for Jesus, we can appreciate the sacrifice it took for him to risk everything. While he has sacrificed the most for us, others have made sacrifices to bring us a better life. Several hundred years ago, many people risked their lives for America to become a free nation. If you live in the United States of America as I do, then hopefully, you realize that we live in a truly amazing country.

There's something to be said about having freedom. Sometimes we are appreciative of this, but truly we are not thankful *enough*. Instead, we get caught up in the day-to-day worries of this world. I've been very guilty of it myself many times in the past. Jesus says in Matthew 6:34, "Therefore do not worry about tomorrow, for tomorrow will worry about itself. Each day has enough trouble of its own."

Biblical Lesson: God wants us to be diligent planners and trust in him. It is fine to prepare out your day with work, school, and family schedules and priorities. However, we cannot stress about the unexpected because we are letting worries become a bigger focus than the Lord.

Gratitude Can Set Us Free

Most of the time, our brains are naturally and subconsciously thinking negatively as we try to survive and protect ourselves. If we constantly have our dukes up expecting something bad to happen, it is no wonder that so many of us struggle with deep depression and anxiety issues; but true gratitude can help. Remember, I had gradually crawled out of my hole of anxiety when I truly focused on what I was grateful for in my life. In Hebrews 12:28, it states, "Therefore, since we are receiving a kingdom that cannot be shaken, let us be thankful, and so worship God acceptably with reverence and awe."

Biblical Lesson: There are an infinite number of things we can be thankful for with the Lord. Everything good comes from above. We can be thankful for blessings in our life such as family, friends, food, shelter, and a home. In addition, we can be thankful for providing second chances and forgiving us, answering prayer requests, and watching over us.

To inherit God's unshakable kingdom, we first have to accept Jesus, and once we do, we have much to be thankful for. His Word states in Romans 10:9–10, "If you declare with your mouth, 'Jesus is Lord,' and believe in your heart that God raised him from the dead, you will be saved. For it is with your heart that you believe and are justified, and it is with your mouth that you profess your faith and are saved."

Biblical Lesson: This verse is worth more than anything in the entire universe! Believe in Jesus with all your heart, and you will reap a glorious and unshakable heaven! We should be thankful for this every single day. Any day could be our last, so let's begin by being grateful and joyous for our heavenly Father.

What We Have to be Thankful For

Everyone had a beginning by being born into this world, and any day we could pass away. So we need to live each day with gratitude for our own lives and for the lives of others. Every child of God is a blessing, and we should treat everyone as such. The birth of every single one of us, God's precious gift, is a wonderful reminder of his love and grace. The Word says in Psalm 139:13–16, "For you created my inmost being; you knit me together in my mother's womb. I praise you because I am fearfully and wonderfully made; your works are wonderful, I know that full well. My frame was not hidden from you when I was made in the secret place, when I was woven together in the depths of the earth. Your eyes saw my unformed body; all the days ordained for me were written in your book before one of them came to be."

Biblical Lesson: From the very beginning, God formed us, nurtures us, watches over us, and displays a love for us that is unmatched. Before we learned to walk, talk, see, hear, feel, taste, smell, think, and process our surroundings, the Lord was always with us, just as he is today. Whether you choose to receive and absorb his love and reciprocate, it is up to you, but it's always available regardless of how much we have sinned in our lives.

We may live in dark times, but we would have nothing if we ceased to exist. In James 1:17–18, the Lord said, "Every good and perfect gift is from above, coming down from the Father of the heavenly lights, who does not change like shifting shadows. He chose to give us birth through the word of truth, that we might be a kind of firstfruits of all he created." With God, there will always be light in the darkness, and the light will always persevere and outshine the darkness.

Biblical Lesson: God is our rock, which is always stable. He is the same in the past, present, and future. The Lord will always be great and will always be our Savior. When we follow his plans for our lives, it will be a much straighter and easier path to guide us. Then we can discern the light from the darkness when making choices.

If we can identify them, we will see the Lord brought light to an infinite number of things in our lives, and we can show gratitude to the Lord. One of those is healing and protection.

I cannot count how many times I have almost hit a deer with my car. One bad collision could send the deer through my windshield and kill me instantly. I'm extremely thankful for every near miss. Also, I've had some minor health issues from time to time that I'm grateful were not worse. In first grade, I slit my pinky finger with an X-ACTO knife, and the blood poured everywhere. The ER doctors said if the knife had gone about an eighth of an inch deeper, they would have had to amputate my finger. In the eighth grade, I injured my wrist while playing football. Even though I will forever feel the wrist injury effects, I am reminded in each instance that the Lord is always with me to help me heal and move forward. A year ago, I was hit by a softball while playing a game with my family. I suffered a concussion and lost a tooth, but I could have easily lost more teeth, broken my jaw or nose, fractured other bones, or even been killed.

Everyone faces trials and tribulations in different forms in their lives. We can take solace that God is right by our side when someone faces cancer, a family member dies, or someone experiences horrible trauma. In Isaiah 41:10, the Lord says, "So do not fear, for I am with you; do not be dismayed, for I am your God. I will strengthen you and help you; I will uphold you with my righteous right hand." Everyone needs the comforting presence that comes from knowing Jesus. We have a choice in this world. All of us can choose to be thankful no matter what life throws our way. However, some of us allow our circumstances to dictate our lives and darken our hearts. No matter what strikes us in the world, we will overcome it. In Psalm 34:19, it states, "The righteous person may have many troubles, but the Lord delivers him from them all."

Biblical Lesson: Regardless of our challenges, we can be thankful to Jesus, no matter what. Everyone experiences difficult circumstances from time to time. It's easy to get tired of dealing with everyday problems. Change your focus and be thankful that God can help push you through those difficult times.

Another area we can show gratitude for is redemption. We have all sinned in various forms and degrees. All of us have made mistakes, and we can use these to grow in our walk with Christ. Reflect on specific times when you were in a very bad place spiritually. What steps did you take to become successful and overcome your issues? Did you specifically incorporate the Lord? When you encounter bad times in the future, look at the successes you have had as encouragement and motivation and see how you can seek God during difficult times.

Something else we should always be thankful for is our most basic living needs. It's easy to forget about these, but safety, food, and shelter are all so important in our lives. I would put something else in that group, which would be family. When one thinks of a home, what would it be without family? We are blessed just to have a family, a roof over our heads, and food to put on the table. Family provides this comfort and safety. If you ever become scared that you won't be able to feed your family or stay in a safe place, know that he cares for everything on this planet. In Luke 12:24, Jesus said, "Consider the ravens: They do not sow or reap, they have no storeroom or barn; yet God feeds them. And how much more valuable you are than birds!" It's very easy to think about the next meal or having enough money to pay off the mortgage, yet the Lord wants us to use some caution. His Word states in Hebrews 13:5, "Keep your lives free from the love of money and be content with what you have, because God has said, 'Never will I leave you; never will I forsake you.'"

Biblical Lesson: There can be something wonderful to live a simple life with just the bare necessities instead of chasing the Benjamins. Whether someone is a millionaire or struggling to make ends meet, we can all be a blessing to others.

Remember: Make a conscious decision to be thankful for tough situations rather than be engulfed in your sufferings. Every good thing in your life is worth being thankful for, including the most basic living needs.

Take Action: Stop trying to protect yourself. Use your tough circumstances as a way to be thankful by drawing closer to the Lord. Count your blessings, and then find a way to share what you are thankful for with others.

CHAPTER 6
FRESH

You might see the title of this chapter and think, *What in the world is this about?* Well, consider that when you go to the produce and deli sections, you look for the freshest fruit, vegetables, and meat. Why would anyone buy food that would harm their family and make them sick?

Most people in their right mind wouldn't entertain such an idea. Produce only has a limited shelf life, so time is of the essence if we want to consume healthy food. Just like food has an expiration date, so do all people. Our time on this earth is so precious and limited, and it's true we only get one shot at it. We cannot postpone and procrastinate spreading the good news of the gospel.

Live Like You Have an Expiration Date

If we treated every day as our last day, we would have a greater sense of urgency. I'm far from perfect in this area and certainly feel like I'm lacking most of the time. However, the biggest difference for me is that it's something that I *strive for*. This whole concept of comparing our short lives to produce may seem corny—pun intended—but I really believe the similarities are important.

Many things in this world are out of our control. One of the variables we have some influence on is time but, more specifically, what we can do to help others *today*! Numerous Bible verses stress the importance of time in our faith journey. In Romans 13:11, the Lord said, "And do this, understanding the present time: The hour has already come for you to wake up from your slumber, because our salvation is nearer now than when we first believed." If that's not a wake-up call, then I don't know what is.

Biblical Lesson: Any day could be our last. Today, not tomorrow, is the day when we need to reach out to God asking for spiritual guidance if we are uncertain of our path. Even if you don't have clarity, jump right in and don't hesitate. Don't let your anxiety and depression stop you from serving others.

Anxiety made it difficult to get out of bed, survive the workday, and complete basic chores. Sometimes I only looked forward to hitting the sack. We weren't created to snooze the day away, even though that may sound appealing sometimes. Instead, we must get off the couch, adjust our focus, look at where our priorities truly are, and get our hands ready to move hearts towards the light today. Scripture states in 2 Corinthians 6:2, "For he says, 'In the time of my favor I heard you, and in the day of salvation I helped you.' I tell you, now is the time of God's favor, now is the day of salvation."

Biblical Lesson: The Lord is always ready to help us when we invite him into our lives. There shouldn't be a when. Today, not tomorrow, is when we should start putting God first in everything we do. Don't miss your chance since any day it could be too late.

Time and time again, the Lord has blessed us, taken care of us, loved us, and been good to us when we didn't even recognize it. Today, we need to show thanks to the great I Am. His plan for us is clear. His Word states in 1 John 2:17, "The world and its desires pass away, but whoever does the will of God lives forever."

Biblical Lesson: Be careful with obsessions of material items and evil desires. They may seem real enjoyable now, but they will expire and blow away in time. Recognize these things are only temporary, and focus instead of what is permanent and everlasting - the love of God.

Living with a Fresh Mindset

To do his will by being followers of Christ, we need to have a *fresh* mindset in this evil world. Where are we focusing our attention? Sometimes having a fresh mindset means you don't get caught up in the negativities in the media or what others are saying. Occasionally, I will just pass the time following message board comments in news articles and on sports websites. People create anonymous usernames where they can spew garbage at others, being disrespectful, and making fun of others all by hiding behind a computer screen. Most of these things wouldn't be said if they were face-to-face. I often have to remind myself to stay away from such nonsense. One verse that speaks to this is in Romans 12:2 stating, "Do not conform to the pattern of this world, but be transformed by the renewing of your mind. Then you will be able to test and approve what God's will is—his good, pleasing and perfect will."

Biblical Lesson: Our world is broken, and with that comes a lot of evil where some people are criminal, immoral, and selfish. These things are not at all what God's Word teaches us. This is exactly why we need daily reminders to pray and connect with Jesus so we can be led by the Holy Spirit.

The patterns of this world are overwhelming, and sometimes these are the only things we feel. Our connection to Jesus is around, but we keep our Savior in the background and at a distance. Our concerns became entangled in earthly matters, ones that we become stressed out about that will only disappear with time. Our temporary desires trump God's will, which is permanent and forever. We must forcibly shift our mindset. In Romans 8:12–13, his Word says, "Therefore, brothers and sisters, we have an obligation—but it is not to the flesh, to live according to it. For if you live according to the flesh, you will die; but if by the Spirit you put to death the misdeeds of the body, you will live."

Biblical Lesson: To live though the Holy Spirit means we must stop giving into our fleshly desires. We will constantly have strong urges in the beginning, but Jesus can help us learn to eventually cast it aside. It will be easier when we recognize these temptations as temporary and trivial in comparison to spiritual matters.

How, then, do we refrain from following the sinful cravings that are ingrained in us? Starve them and stop giving them attention. His Word says in 2 Timothy 2:22, "Flee the evil desires of youth and pursue righteousness, faith, love, and peace, along with those who call on the Lord out of a pure heart." Believe me, it will hurt badly, and the process could be drawn out. It will probably drive you crazy at times. This uncomfortable pain will be worth it because it will draw us closer to Jesus. He experienced suffering in his life too. If it all seems too unbearable, take heart in what the Lord said in 1 Corinthians 10:13, "No temptation has overtaken you except what is common to mankind. And God is faithful; he will not let you be tempted beyond what you can bear. But when you are tempted, he will also provide a way out so that you can endure it."

Biblical Lesson: When we are hurting mentally, physically, and spiritually, it is easy to give in to the discomfort and break down internally. In these trying times, resist and resist even more. Turn to God for self-discipline to turn your back from these urges.

We all become accustomed to daily habits that we do naturally, each facing our own sinful habits. It is time to stop the bleeding of our sinful ways, to rip off the chains of bondage we have to our earthly desires that hold us back. In Colossians 3:5, the Lord said, "Put to death, therefore, whatever belongs to your earthly nature: sexual immorality, impurity, lust, evil desires and greed, which is idolatry." We can all start somewhere.

Changing our Contaminated Habits

Several years ago, my anxiety consumed me. No matter what activities I was involved in, it was always in the back of my mind. Even on good days when I was very happy, my body still felt the long-term effects of anxiety. This entailed feeling wired all the time and a slightly elevated heart rate, sleep difficulties, irritability, and more. It was an uncomfortable feeling that never left me.

Understandably, every day I was looking for ways to ease, improve, or eliminate those feelings. For example, I would take numerous hot baths and showers each day, practice slow breathing routines, do yoga, meditate, bite my fingernails, and work out. While I would sit down on the couch, I constantly researched my anxiety and what could be wrong with me. It was a never-ending, vicious cycle. I visited hundreds of websites through the years researching many things—anxiety prevention, triggers, symptoms, medication, chemical imbalances, and endorphins. Sometimes I would pray, but many times I tried to figure out my issues on my own instead of trusting in God.

My mindset was contaminated, far from being fresh. It was so focused on finding comfort in any way possible, a temporary gratification that won't matter down the road. I could have directed my attention to God's will and his plan for me, which does matter down the road. Instead, I became lost in my own affairs. As a result, I pitied myself, dug a deeper hole, and prolonged my own suffering.

As I mentioned earlier, when I finally learned to change my focus by putting others first, only then did my anxiety and depression gradually disappear. I chose a fresh mindset, focusing on what mattered before it expired. Through it all, I'm thankful for all the pain and suffering that I experienced. Because of it, I have come much closer to the Lord because I've learned to rely on him and find peace instead of figuring out life by myself.

Fresh Responses

We also need a fresh mindset with how we respond to those who hurt us. We do not want to go to the grave having a beef with others. We could have a lifetime of grudges. It's easy to focus on revenge or remain bitter towards those who verbally or physically assaulted us. In Romans 12:17–21, the Lord said,

> "Do not repay anyone evil for evil. Be careful to do what is right in the eyes of everyone. If it is possible,

as far as it depends on you, live at peace with everyone. Do not take revenge, my dear friends, but leave room for God's wrath, for it is written: 'It is mine to avenge; I will repay,' says the Lord. On the contrary: 'If your enemy is hungry, feed him; if he is thirsty, give him something to drink. In doing this, you will heap burning coals on his head.' Do not be overcome by evil, but overcome evil with good."

Biblical Lesson: The world, society, and the media would tell you to punch that person back, talk negatively about that individual, and seek payback in any form or fashion. Essentially, we are to love our enemies regardless of what crimes they have committed against us. In addition, we are not to judge others as only our heavenly Father has this right, or else we will be judged. We can be a shining light in this world no matter what darkness we have faced. When all is said and done, we will not be remembered for our personal accomplishments but how we live for Jesus, and a prime example is when we have suffered on account of others.

Fresh Mindset in Spreading God's Word

We need to be bold to spread God's Word. Instead, we sometimes act like chickens. Basically, we're behaving like a bunch of nervous birds too worried about what the rest of the world thinks. This used to be me. Mornings were always the hardest because this was when I would experience the most anxiety. I was so concerned about how the world perceived me and, thus, how I could survive the day. Once evenings arrived, I was much more relaxed and comfortable, which probably was because I didn't have to deal with people and their expectations of me.

Fear has got to stop robbing us of joy and in spreading that joy. It doesn't have to be this way. The Lord said in 1 John 4:18–19, "There is no fear in love. But perfect love drives out fear, because fear has to do with punishment. The one who fears is not made perfect in love. We love because he first loved us." If we want to free ourselves of fear, we need to bow down and surrender to God and then lift others up in love. Finally, we were not created in God's image to be people pleasers. We were made to be God pleasers! Stop fearing what others think of you, but fear the Lord. You are not a slave to any one person and their expectations of you. The Lord said in Romans 13:8 (ESV), "Owe no one anything, except to love each other, for the one who loves another has fulfilled the law."

Biblical Lesson: Surely we need to be God pleasers by being a blessing to all his children regardless of past hurt some of our enemies have brought to us. This is the beginning of wisdom that our world surely needs more of.

Remember: Purposefully recognize your fleshly desires, make them secondary motives, and make room for God's will in your life front and center.

Take Action: Today is the day we spread the news of the gospel. Stop procrastinating and making excuses.

CHAPTER 7
HUMILITY

One thing about keeping a fresh mindset is about humility, and this has been one of the hardest subjects for me to address as I grow closer to Jesus. I've never been arrogant, cocky, or boastful. Generally, I've been the one who is quiet and avoids confrontations. I've never been in a physical fight. But this doesn't mean that quiet, shy individuals like me can't have some hidden pride issues. It took decades for ugliness to be uncovered and identified in my life.

Be Humble Enough to Listen to the Other Side

There are plenty of things we have to learn to become humble about. First things first—for some time, my heart has been hurting to see the state our country is in. Whether it is politics, sports, school, or community-related, we cannot continue to throw shade at those who have different backgrounds, upbringings, or viewpoints. Different opinions lately have caused more hostility than usual. So many want to be identified with belonging to a certain group. This is fine with the caveat that we love the other side, respect them, listen and not just hear, meet in the middle or find common ground, collaborate, and develop meaningful solutions together. These things are certainly a good starting point, but Jesus wants us to go even further. In 2 Chronicles 7:14, the Lord said, "If my people, who are called by my name, will humble themselves and pray and seek my face and turn from their wicked ways, then I will hear from heaven, and I will forgive their sin and will heal their land."

Biblical Lesson: When we pray for God's guidance in solving today's issues, it will go a long way when we align it with his will. It starts by showing humility when admitting our mistakes and asking for forgiveness. Then we can pray for wisdom in learning God's will for our life.

Be Humble Enough to Allow Jesus In

Many people struggle with issues because we try to figure them out by ourselves. When we leave Jesus out of the equation, it can cause a real mess. A lot of instability may ensue. I was always one to overanalyze situations, scrutinize them, and develop my own conclusions on how to solve problems.

When it came to figuring out how to crush my debilitating anxiety issues, I finally realized that I couldn't figure things out on my own. There was no way I could have made it on my own. It wasn't until I stopped focusing on myself that I got better.

The bottom line was I needed to count on the Lord. The answer was simple—I needed to follow Jesus and not get lost on my own path. This message couldn't be any clearer than in God's Word in 1 Peter 2:21: "To this you were called, because Christ suffered for you, leaving you an example, that you should follow in his steps."

Biblical Lesson: This is an open invitation to know Jesus and draw closer to him. We need to take a leap of faith to become closer to our Savior significantly. With that will sometimes come pain and discomfort. Are you willing to sacrifice for Christ when he died for your sins on the cross? It is a deeply spiritual yet personal question that requires intimate reflection. If we can develop even an ounce of the same burning desire and thirst as Paul the apostle, then we can truly move mountains with Jesus by our side.

Humble in Your Suffering

In Philippians 3:10, Paul wrote, "I want to know Christ—yes, to know the power of his resurrection and participation in his sufferings, becoming like him in his death."

Biblical Lesson: If we want to truly understand our Savior and get closer to him, then we will have to step out of our comfort zone. We may have to sacrifice majorly to accomplish this. Knowing Jesus on a far deeper level is more than worth it.

This brings us to the crippling issue of anxiety. If you have ever, like me, felt terrified, frozen, crippled, obsessed, hopeless, sick, nauseous, and misguided, then you are not alone. Many of these feelings are heightened when we don't feel as close to the Lord. We have to learn to be comfortable with the uncomfortable. This is the suffering. Don't fight it. It will be all right. You were born for this. It's in your DNA. These words are echoed again by Paul in Philippians 1:29: "For it has been granted to you on behalf of Christ not only to believe in him, but also to suffer for him." Some may be skeptical of such thinking. God's will is not from this world. We should take comfort that there is a reason for the suffering. Scripture in 2 Corinthians 1:4–5 states, "Who comforts us in all our troubles, so that we can comfort those in any trouble with the comfort we ourselves receive from God. For just as we share abundantly in the sufferings of Christ, so also our comfort abounds through Christ."

Biblical Lesson: One way we can be effective in serving others is simply by relating to others. When we help those suffering from something that previously hurt us, then it will be easier for dialogue to occur. In addition, we may move hearts closer to Christ when we set a positive example.

We are a beautiful gift from our Creator made to move hearts in times of both celebration and suffering. Every life is precious, and all of us need to show the love of God to each other when we are at our best and worst. And we need to do it today, not on our terms when it's convenient! Whether it's by our hands or our words, we can spread the love of God. In the end, our suffering will not only benefit the Lord but our own personal growth too. In Romans 5:3–4, Scripture states, "Not only so, but we also glory in our sufferings, because we know that suffering produces perseverance; perseverance, character; and character, hope."

Biblical Lesson: As we grow our trust in God, we also need to develop characteristics that are necessary to conquer our anxieties and fears. Hope in Christ gives us a reason to live and love others. Character and perseverance help us to show integrity when in challenging circumstances.

Let Go of Ego and Pride

Often, we don't want to embark on something that may fail. When it was time for me to apply to colleges, I didn't apply to the University of Michigan, my favorite school, for fear of being rejected. I didn't want to be embarrassed. My grade point average was exceptional, but my ACT standardized test scores were below the average of students that met admissions standards. So, guess what? I applied to three other in-state schools and was accepted to each of them. As I look back, I know that I took the easy way out instead of trying to live out my dream. I could have tried to score higher on my ACT to improve my chances of getting accepted at the University of Michigan. I chickened out. How will we ever grow spiritually, personally, and professionally if we are afraid of failure? Without failure, we will never grow and learn. There's something to be said for hitting a low point and growing from there. In Proverbs 29:23, his Word says, "Pride brings a person low, but the lowly in spirit gain honor."

Biblical Lesson: Pride can bring us all to a fall. For some, it may be growing pains. If we become humble deep in our hearts while asking for forgiveness and giving thanks, then we will see our weaknesses as an extraordinary opportunity to allow God to move into our lives to fill the gaps we may not have even realized existed.

Our Own Desires Should Not Trump God's Will

There is absolutely nothing wrong with pursuing something that makes us happy. However, if God has created each of us with specific talents, skills, and abilities to be a blessing towards others, then who are we to fight what amazing plans the Lord has for us? Why question it? For most of my life, my focus has primarily been centered on my career. In the past, my prayers often revolved around jobs and work. It saddens me that I didn't consider asking the Lord more often how I could make a difference for his children.

Many times I did what was best for me, not the Lord. For example, I used to hold a great nonprofit position that promoted the gift of life, yet I quit the job and gave up on it too early for selfish reasons. My job was to be a community relations associate, promoting eye, organ, and tissue donation. Essentially, I was advocating for helping others and saving lives. It was something that I enjoyed, yet when I reflect on that time, it was as if I wanted it not to work. Eventually, I thought that I was "too cool" to be working most weekends, and then when I went on vacation to Texas and came back home, I decided I would move out there.

I was blessed to be in a role serving others and helping to save lives, but I lost sight of the mission. Instead, I followed my own desire and moved away from God's will. When I lived in Texas, I was roommates with a cousin who is basically my brother, so I had a great time with him out there, and he was amazing. At the end of the day, I moved back to Michigan because I realized I missed home, and I grew tired of the bar scene in my twenties. After moving back home, I hit rock bottom and went through waves of anxiety and depression.

I firmly believe a lot of this pain and suffering was a result of not following God. When God is absent from our lives, a lot of anxiety may result. I finally realized I needed to make some changes for a spiritual breakthrough. They gradually worked because I took some time to find myself, and after making necessary changes in my life, I met my beautiful wife. I have no regrets about my journey because the ups and downs got me to where I am today.

Even though this may have all been a part of the plan, it doesn't mean that my desires weren't above God's will at the time. The Lord makes such an important point in Galatians 5:13–15 when he said, "You, my brothers and sisters, were called to be free. But do not use your freedom to indulge the flesh; rather, serve one another humbly in love. For the entire law is fulfilled in keeping this one command: 'Love your neighbor as yourself.' If you bite and devour each other, watch out or you will be destroyed by each other."

Biblical Lesson: Don't take advantage of the freedom we were given when Christ died for our sins. Love God and all his children first. If we decide to sin often, then we will fall in bondage to the devil and move away from the Lord.

Sometimes it's important to take a step back before we make a life-changing decision, reflect on it, pray to the Lord, and examine if it really aligns with God's plans for our lives. Should we choose to go on our own path, then we are asking for major trouble when we face these overwhelming mountains and hurdles. When we do this, we are acting in defiance of the Lord and must realize that we may be held accountable for our selfish, sinful acts. In Galatians 5:19-21, God said, "The acts of the flesh are obvious: sexual immorality, impurity and debauchery; idolatry and witchcraft; hatred, discord, jealousy, fits of rage, selfish ambition, dissensions, factions and envy; drunkenness, orgies, and the like. I warn you, as I did before, that those who live like this will not inherit the kingdom of God."

Biblical Lesson: It's a fact that we are all sinners. We must reject the evil temptations, seek forgiveness, humble ourselves, and draw closer to the Lord. Everyday we must try to be led by the Holy Spirit.

Many times when we aren't able to accomplish our desires that originate from the flesh, we can develop all kinds of emotions. We may feel stressed, depressed, angry, jealous, empty, crazy, and confused. People will wonder why their wishes aren't coming true, and then they become frustrated should their prayers not be answered to their liking. Our cravings for food, sex, money, sleep, fame, honor, trophies, drugs, and alcohol can become overwhelming, and we become glued to these temporary desires.

Honoring God through Our Bodies

Believe it or not, our body is not our own because Jesus paid the ultimate price for it. In 1 Corinthians 6:19–20, Scripture said, "Do you not know that your bodies are temples of the Holy Spirit, who is in you, whom you have received from God? You are not your own; you were bought at a price. Therefore honor God with your bodies." I go through many phases where I eat healthily, and then others where I indulge and eat to my heart's content. It's very difficult to stay committed, so you may need to ask for help from above.

Biblical Lesson: If we are reborn and consider ourselves followers of Christ, then we must truly follow what he commands. We must be careful with what we do, and commit to serving him and helping others.

Honoring God with Our Prayers

Just as we should honor God with our bodies, we should also honor him with our prayers. In our prayers, we should focus on humility, which entails bowing down to the only worthy one, our almighty God. The Lord said in 1 John 5:14–15, "This is the confidence we have in approaching God: that if we ask anything according to his will, he hears us. And if we know that he hears us—whatever we ask—we know that we have what we asked of him."

Biblical Lesson: When we pray, we should pour our hearts out in both good and bad times. Effective prayer involves developing a deeper relationship with God daily. In the past, I felt that I was so stuck in a severe anxious state that it was just a one-sided connection, with me desperately crying out to the Lord. It took some time to realize that I needed to listen to God, have confidence and trust in the Lord, and pray in a way asking to live out God's plans for me according to his will. When we do that, we can gradually learn about the amazing grace and peace that comes from knowing Jesus.

Remember: Christ suffered not only so we may be free but also as an example. So to truly follow him, we must also learn how to suffer for him as well. It's not easy to show humility to others because, often, our pride gets in the way.

Take Action: We must bow down and humble ourselves and recognize that the ultimate price was paid for us, so we must honor the Lord with our bodies, heart, mind, and soul.

CHAPTER 8
TRUTH

Many know from experience that anxiety and depression rob people of joy. It's one of the numerous tools Satan utilizes to cause discord in our lives. Scripture references that the devil only comes to steal, kill, and destroy. Anxiety is a weapon of fear stirring in our hearts and minds. It's one fabricated on destructive lies. No longer does anxiety need to control our lives. There is only one truth, Jesus Christ.

For believers, the most important thing one can learn and apply to their lives is that Jesus Christ is the answer, the truth, and the foundation on which we must live our lives. Christ is the only rock we should rely on. In John 14:6, Scripture says, "Jesus answered, 'I am the way and the truth and the life. No one comes to the Father except through me.'"

Biblical Lesson: We need to absorb this life-changing verse and look at how we are living our lives, align our hearts with Christ, and transform our hearts and minds so that Jesus is the cornerstone of our actions, conversations, thoughts, and motives. For many, it is a decision we have to make as we approach each day.

One question we can all ask is, How do we want to be remembered? Is it to be in a famous rock band? What about being the best salesperson ever? Could it be becoming the world's most famous athlete? The true question is, Are these pursuits number one in our hearts, or is it really Jesus? Many of us will want to be remembered for the accomplishments attached to our first and last names. Yet when our day comes, all that matters is what differences and impact we made in the name of Jesus. This will be our legacy—how we glorified the name of our almighty God, Jesus Christ, and the Holy Spirit.

When I made the shift from obsessing about myself to focusing on helping others, thanks to my wife's wisdom, it was very hard for me. The challenge of that shift truly showed how deep my problems were. It illustrated how massive a divide was created between my heart's desires compared to God's will for me. My rock bottom was also my turning point.

The turnaround resulted because I finally followed the truth of putting Jesus first. This also meant putting his children first. By doing this, the weight of my selfish burdens was lifted. I was unchained and set free. When I started shining the light on others, his name was glorified. By keeping all my burdens inside, it created instability and real darkness that manifested itself through severe anxiety and depression.

Not only did my anxiety begin to get better nearly every day but my wife and I were blessed with the news that she was pregnant. We were so thankful for such glorious news because we had been trying to have a baby for about three years after our miscarriage. The pregnancy went well, and now my wife and I have two amazing little girls. Life has been much easier taking care of two little ones (a labor-intensive process that is a blessing) without the darkness that severe OCD and anxiety can bring. Without God, none of this would have been possible. Every good thing comes from above. Everything in God's will happens for a reason.

From the bottom of my heart, I believe the Lord was using this miracle as a sign that following him is the *only* way. If we want to see our Father in heaven, then living our own way is not going to cut it. It will take constant reminders because every day that we wake up, we will see worldly concerns that try to grab our attention and distract us from God's message. We need to remember the important truths of the gospel.

Freedom from Pressures

When we recognize Jesus and what he stood for, we have freedom in Christ. We are free from the pressures to perform, so then why do we agonize and torment ourselves to perform? Often it is because we try to be people pleasers. In other cases, we ourselves apply these pressures because we are prioritizing our goals over those of God. When I was stuck in my anxious rut, I constantly brainstormed and researched hundreds of ways to escape the hell-like feelings. One uncomfortable feeling I sometimes had was being fearful of others' thoughts and expectations of me. Instead, it is important to love and care for people and not get caught up in unreasonable expectations. Fear should not come from other people. Instead, there should be fear that is about respect and reverence for God. Scripture says in Psalm 33:18–19, "But the eyes of the Lord are on those who fear him, on those whose hope is in his unfailing love, to deliver them from death and keep them alive in famine."

Biblical Lesson: God gives blessings to those who have the utmost admiration, love, and trust in him. They will never perish. This is exactly why we should focus far more on the Lord than trying to be a people pleaser.

If we set our eyes on the Lord, then only he will be our number one priority. From there, we can love all his children by being a Christlike example. After that, we can still try to perform our best with our job, our role as a parent, friend, or teacher, or other supporting or leadership responsibilities. This is freedom from earthly pressures.

We Must Live by Faith

Regardless of how horrific the pain and agony we are feeling at the moment, we must remember that this is all temporary. We were given five senses, but this doesn't give us the big picture. We have tunnel vision and cannot experience the glory of heaven because it is unseen. The Lord said in 2 Corinthians 5:7, "For we live by faith, not by sight."

Biblical Lesson: Our world is a very scary place. If we only live by sight, then our lives would be far less enjoyable and all joy might be drained from us. Our sight is extremely limited, so we will not pick up on all the amazing things the Lord does for his children.

We will hit a dead-end if we do not believe. And if we do believe in Jesus Christ, then we must believe with all our hearts. Having even a shred of doubt will hurt whatever faith we do have, especially when we are praying to the Lord. Scripture says in James 1:5–8, "If any of you lacks wisdom, you should ask God, who gives generously to all without finding fault, and it will be given to you. But when you ask, you must believe and not doubt, because the one who doubts is like a wave of the sea, blown and tossed by the wind. That person should not expect to receive anything from the Lord. Such a person is double-minded and unstable in all they do." This verse is stating that we must believe that God can supply us with all our needs no matter what we are facing.

Biblical Lesson: We must learn to keep our faith stable and grounded. Any shred of doubt will put a major dent in our faith and make it as unpredictable as the wind. Turn to Christ to solidify our faith.

I wonder how many times I asked for something in prayer but my anxiety loomed larger than my faith in the Lord.

While I always felt that I had faith, often, all I knew were the emotions I was feeling. Whatever source or trigger initiating my anxiety would loom larger than my faith in God. Needless to say, severe anxiety made it very difficult to operate.

My anxiety was blocking my faith. It was there; I just couldn't reach it. And just like with all people, sometimes life circumstances reduced my faith, but in Matthew 17:20, Jesus spoke to those with little faith: "Because you have so little faith. Truly I tell you, if you have faith as small as a mustard seed, you can say to this mountain, 'Move from here to there,' and it will move. Nothing will be impossible for you."

Biblical Lesson: Even an ounce of faith can turn things in the right direction. If we desire to continually grow our relationship with Jesus, then we must continue to press on and build on our faith. The more we draw into the Lord, the greater the impact our prayers can be answered according to God's will.

We Must Have a Passion for Christ

Our relationship with the Lord will only go as far as our hearts will take us. Do you wake up every morning wondering what your purpose might be? Are you discouraged or uninterested in pursuing Jesus? Are you stuck or caught up in the stresses of this world?

Most people would have said yes to at least one or more of these questions at some point. For Jesus to move the needle in our lives, we need to have a passion for him. It is a constant pursuit that requires every fiber of our bodies to be invested. In Jeremiah 29:13, Scripture says, "You will seek me and find me when you seek me with all your heart." The key word here is *all*, and God is serious when he states this. Why should the Lord be placed on the back burner? Isn't he worth so much more than being noticed from time to time? I've been guilty of this like so many. Jesus said in Psalm 34:10, "The lions may grow weak and hungry, but those who seek the Lord lack no good thing."

Biblical Lesson: I truly believe that all humans, like even courageous lions, will fall apart and become nothing without Jesus because we rip each other to shreds, attempt to live life on our own, and pursue our fleshly desires first. Without being led by the Holy Spirit, we will starve ourselves of righteousness because we are being distracted by the devil and not following the truth of God's calling.

We All Need Repentance

We have all sinned, made mistakes, screwed up royally, and fallen short of the glory of God. He cares deeply about us bowing and taking a knee and confessing. In Luke 15:7, Jesus said, "I tell you that in the same way there will be more rejoicing in heaven over one sinner who repents than over ninety-nine righteous persons who do not need to repent."

Biblical Lesson: By repenting, we can use this to draw closer to him. A lot of depression and anxiety has resulted from our mistakes and sins. By repenting, we can release all this to our Savior so we can find that peace. We must repent, learn our lesson, forgive ourselves, and finally move on. We don't need to pour salt in our own wounds.

Many times we repent but turn back to our wicked ways. In 2 Chronicles 7:14, the Lord said, "If my people, who are called by my name, will humble themselves and pray and seek my face and turn from their wicked ways, then I will hear from heaven, and I will forgive their sin and will heal their land."

Biblical Lesson: No one is perfect except for God. It is incredible the amazing grace he gives us. While we will never be perfect, we should still strive for perfection. The key is to repent, ask for forgiveness, seek God's wisdom, and try numerous times to get better.

We Need to Love Each Other

Our nation would not have as much hardship if we loved each other and didn't view others with different beliefs or backgrounds as the enemy. After all, we were all created by God. We need to love and respect those who we perceive to be different than us on the surface, when in reality, we all have a heartbeat, breathe the same air, survive by drinking water, and bleed no differently, among many other things. By loving others, following his ways, and putting our trust in the Lord, this is when we can truly call ourselves children of God.

Embrace Your Imperfections and Turn to Christ

This includes daily struggles with illnesses like OCD, anxiety, and depression. Anything like this can make living each day difficult and hopeless. So often, my struggles with anxiety felt like never-ending suffering. However, God has purposes for your hardships. In Matthew 11:28–30, the Lord said, "Come to me, all you who are weary and burdened, and I will give you rest. Take my yoke upon you and learn from me, for I am gentle and humble in heart, and you will find rest for your souls. For my yoke is easy and my burden is light."

Biblical Lesson: When we are suffering, we have a choice to turn to Christ. There is always an open invitation to follow Christ, and we have the freedom to choose. Ultimately, we are the ones who have to make it, which will require us to humble ourselves in turning to God and never turning back. Sometimes it may take months or even years before we learn to finally let go. It will be all right. You are never alone with Jesus.

Remember: You have an open invitation to always follow the Lord. All you need to do is step through this door to begin this journey.

Take Action: Dive deep by asking the Lord for wisdom on which lies have distracted you from these truths, and seek Jesus with every fiber in your body to build on this relationship daily.

CHAPTER 9
GENTLE

In this world, we are prone to attacks on all different fronts. It doesn't matter if it's while we are fighting for our lives during our lowest point or getting a tan on the beach. It's fair to say that we all have different reactions when we're being threatened. In the past, I would often become sad and agitated when the devil's schemes got under my skin.

Recently, I was on a trip with my family. It was sunny, and I was happy, yet somehow, I could feel the devil trying to pick at me with lies and distractions. My reaction was far different than usual. Out of the blue, I felt that I wanted to attack the lies, distractions, and other stupid devilish schemes. I wanted to punch them in the face. I was wrestling with different feelings and not completely understanding what was happening. Then it seemed like God was sending me a sign, telling me my mindset was too aggressive in this instance. All I wanted to do was fight the devil mentally and provoke the situation even more. The Lord pulled me in, and I remembered a verse: "Take my yoke upon you and learn from me, for I am gentle and humble in heart, and you will find rest for your souls" (Matthew 11:29).

Biblical Lesson: Too often people reluctantly keep their problems to themselves. We hold it back from friends, family, and even, God. Life can be far less stressful when Jesus and a family of believers are there by our side.

It is such a powerful verse that brings peace to your soul, knowing how loving our Lord is. One word instantly calmed my storm: *gentle.* It truly felt like God was telling me to have a gentle mindset. In the days that followed, I felt calmer and more relaxed when challenging situations in life occurred.

Benefits of a Gentle Mindset

As human beings, it's only natural to want to feel safe and protected. It's not uncommon for our survival mode to kick in, and then we prioritize our own safety needs before helping others. When our anxiety makes us feel unsafe, we are uncomfortable and don't want to sit with that discomfort, so we become agitated, restless, jittery, and sometimes too emotional to function well.

A gentle mindset can extinguish any fire in our lives. When all hell breaks loose, we can pour gasoline on it and run for the hills, or we can choose instead to allow our gentleness to be a spiritual tool that destroys evil before it finds its footing.

There is a major reason why the devil is in the ground beneath you, and our heavenly Father, who we worship and find joy in, is above us. Keep the devil in his rightful place by striving to have a gentle mindset at all times. In Philippians 4:5, the Lord said, "Let your gentleness be evident to all. The Lord is near." The very next verse is about anxiety. His Word says in Philippians 4:6–7, "Do not be anxious about anything, but in every situation, by prayer and petition, with thanksgiving, present your requests to God. And the peace of God, which transcends all understanding, will guard your hearts and your minds in Christ Jesus."

Biblical Lesson: The word *understanding* is important in that Scripture because it's pointing out that our understanding is very, very limited in this world. We cannot rely solely on our own experiences. God's peace is light years ahead of what we will ever realize on planet earth. Therefore, we must follow God's Word so that gentleness can guide our minds and hearts. Kindness will erase the fighting and struggling our soul can suffer from.

Being Gentle Helps Others

Jesus went to the cross to die for our sins. All our Savior wants to do is build a relationship with you. He is tenderhearted with all his children. Just as we are loving and kind to newborn babies, why can't we do the same to all God's children?

The Lord wants us to set aside our pride and open up our hearts, perhaps more than we are comfortable with. It may not always be easy, but the Lord wants us to align our hearts with his by loving our neighbors at all times. In Colossians 3:12, his Word states, "Therefore, as God's chosen people, holy and dearly loved, clothe yourselves with compassion, kindness, humility, gentleness, and patience." Our gentleness will teach others to shine God's light on our dark world.

Biblical Lesson: These five qualities can instantly extinguish fires in our world. As God's chosen people, we have a duty to shine light to the darkest places in the world. Even under stressful situations that arise, we may not play it right the first time. The key is to use our failures as opportunities for growth.

This evil world will present many challenges that will test our faith and character. If you suffer severe anxiety, this probably seems like a daily issue. When I was at my worst, I would often get caught up in the pain and discomfort that my body was experiencing from the symptoms of anxiety. The worst entailed my veins always burning and feeling on fire, numerous sleepless nights, heart palpitations, stomachaches, tense muscles, tremors, shortness of breath, brain fog, among other things.

I'm surprised I never truly lashed out at anyone. But I kept the faith all those years, and I don't feel that misery anymore. I still loved and cared for God's people and tried to show kindness to all despite the hell I was enduring. Back then, I believe, I only had half the heart I do now, but I still was kind to others. My career was working as a recruiter and providing job opportunities, so I needed to be nice and helpful. Be gentle to everyone, no matter what anguish you're going through. If I can make it, so can you.

In fact, look at the Lord's greatest commandment, when he states in Mark 12:28–31, "One of the teachers of the law came and heard them debating. Noticing that Jesus had given them a good answer, he asked him, 'Of all the commandments, which is the most important?' 'The most important one,' answered Jesus, 'is this: "Hear, O Israel: The Lord our God, the Lord is one. Love the Lord your God with all your heart and with all your soul and with all your mind and with all your strength." The second is this: "Love your neighbor as yourself. There is no commandment greater than these."'"

Biblical Lesson: We may all fail at certain things in life, but we can always—and I mean always—hold our heads up high if we are gentle-minded and tenderhearted to God's children. Love is always greater than fear, and if we persistently buy into that more and more over time, then our fear will gradually shrivel up.

Remember: A gentle mindset can extinguish any fires you encounter in life, block out all the noise, and allow you to better listen to God's Word on how to handle a tough situation.

Take Action: Use your trauma and pain to your advantage to help out others and bring them closer to Christ. Take the Lord's most important commandments very seriously, and show new ways how to love God and his children.

CHAPTER 10
TRUST

One of the biggest types of anxiety stems from a lack of trust—whether it's with friends, family, coworkers, or God. Typically the saying is you have to earn trust. Then I read that trust is granted, which is probably not often discussed. When I think of trust, I view it as something you choose to give someone based on their credibility.

A relationship with God is the single-most-important relationship that demands your trust. Once that is established, it can trickle down and make it easier to deeply trust your spouse, parents, kids, neighbors, friends, coworkers, and more. What if our trust in God could just be automatic and natural? That is something we could all strive for.

Align Your Heart with God

One thing I've learned from poor decisions on my part is that your heart has to be in the right place and aligned with God first to have much-needed trust with the Lord. Nearly a decade ago, I began tithing for the first time. When I started tithing, I wanted to draw closer to Jesus and help others by giving the first 10 percent. However, unfortunately, I had a secondary motive. I began focusing too much on the blessing that people can receive after tithing.

This became more of a goal than it should have been. When I was tithing, I often prayed to God, asking for his assistance with my career by having my internship turn into a full-time job with benefits. There's certainly nothing wrong with praying to God about your job or career. But I was more concerned about receiving than actually giving. I did not realize how selfish my thinking was.

Fear Is a Lack of Trust

My motivations were influenced by fear. Being fearful is lacking trust and faith in our Creator. The lack of confidence in God will take us on a difficult path, and our struggles will be magnified the further we get from Jesus. Well, when my plan to get a full-time job from my internship didn't come to fruition, I was unemployed for four months while working on my master's. Looking back on it now, I don't think it was that big of a deal. However, it threw me into a deep, dark, depressive state. I became miserable and made life difficult for my close family.

I was focused only on myself. In Acts 20:35, Scripture says, "In everything I did, I showed you that by this kind of hard work we must help the weak, remembering the words the Lord Jesus himself said: 'It is more blessed to give than to receive.'" My heart was focused more on receiving a blessing than actually on giving. Part of this was a lack of trust in potential blessings the Lord would bring to me. If you are one of the millions of people who have severe anxiety, don't give up hope. We have to trust in Jesus because we probably don't always know the root cause deep down. In John 16:33, the Lord said, "I have told you these things, so that in me you may have peace. In this world you will have trouble. But take heart! I have overcome the world."

Biblical Lesson: The world is perishable. It will rot away one day. So will your body and all of your pain, traumas, sorrows, and worries. Your anxieties are only temporary, so focus on detaching yourself from them.

Trusting in Jesus Brings Us Peace

The hard things in our lives can make it challenging to trust. Jesus makes it clear to us that we must follow him in any situation because he is the only way for us to go to heaven. The Lord said in Proverbs 3:5–8, "Trust in the Lord with all your heart and lean not on your own understanding; in all your ways submit to him, and he will make your paths straight.

Do not be wise in your own eyes; fear the Lord and shun evil. This will bring health to your body and nourishment to your bones."

Biblical Lesson: The Lord is looking for a heart of obedience from us. When we stay committed to following Jesus, life will go far more smoothly for us. However, it doesn't mean we won't run into troubles, but we can receive guidance that can help our life.

Typically, we think only about our specific life experiences on earth and don't think of the big picture and heaven above. Our experiences don't have to define us or give us a certain type of identity. The only identity we will be remembered by is how we live for Jesus, so take comfort in this. You don't need to blaze your own trail to survive. The Lord will be with you always. He is an amazing father who loves you more than anyone can ever comprehend, who provides comfort, heals our wounds, protects our soul, and teaches us how to follow his will for us. Nothing will ever compare to the wonderful impact of Christ's love. In Matthew 6:33, the Lord said, "But seek first his kingdom and his righteousness, and all these things will be given to you as well."

Biblical Lesson: God knows exactly what we need before we ask for it. Yet we need to stay committed to God's will for our life rather than focusing on our own needs first.

I have seen in my own life that my selfish acts moved me further away from the truth. I was unfaithful. The Lord was not. He stayed with me the whole time and never left me.

Be Loyal and Trustworthy

The bottom line is that God is loyal and trustworthy. We need to be the same in return.

In challenging times, the devil will try to break your faith. For instance, if a friend or family member betrays you, chances are you may not trust them as much, and the devil may tempt you to lose faith in Christ. In Matthew 10:21–22, Jesus said, "Brother will betray brother to death, and a father his child; children will rebel against their parents and have them put to death. You will be hated by everyone because of me, but the one who stands firm to the end will be saved."

Biblical Lesson: Conflict and evil are inevitable in this world, even amongst family members. Do not allow cruel actions from those close to you to interfere with your faith in Jesus.

Once when I really struggled with friends who hurt me, I felt a sense of betrayal; however, I forgave them and trusted in the Lord. By forgiving them, you are releasing that feeling of bondage because the devil wants you to be hurt.

Trust in Our Suffering

It can be difficult sometimes to follow the Lord when we are suffering. Take, for example, when we lose someone close to us. I can't imagine losing an immediate family member or close friend. Death seems like the end of the world. Yet, in reality, it is a time to finally meet Jesus and our heavenly

Father, whom we have looked up to our entire lives. In John 5:24, the Lord said, "Very truly I tell you, whoever hears my word and believes him who sent me has eternal life and will not be judged but has crossed over from death to life." Jesus cares for all of us deeply and wants us to be comforted in our times of loss and trouble.

Biblical Lesson: Without following Jesus, we will not make it to heaven. There is no other way. Jesus died for our sins, and his purpose is to save those who believe in him. Even when we struggle, our everlasting hope is in his hands.

The Lord wants to help us when we are struggling to plan our future. Often we are left clueless on how to live our lives. Pressures mount from family, friends, society, and ourselves internally. This noise can become deafening. We need not worry, though. In Jeremiah 29:11–13, Scripture states, "'For I know the plans I have for you,' declares the Lord, 'plans to prosper you and not to harm you, plans to give you hope and a future. Then you will call on me and come and pray to me, and I will listen to you. You will seek me and find me when you seek me with all your heart.'"

Biblical Lesson: Once we can learn to block the noise, then we can be still to hear God's word, use it to develop this ever-important relationship, and trust wholly in him. It will be far easier to block out all the noise when we give the Lord our full attention and whole heart.

Remember: Let your trust in God be based on faith, not on your sight. Do not allow your eyes or your personal experiences to deceive you.

Take Action: Seek first the kingdom of God in everything you do, trusting in him as you follow his will for your life. Don't go where the devil is trying to tempt you and destroy you.

CHAPTER 11
FIRE

Many of the things I have mentioned have been reactive ways to stop OCD, anxiety, and depression. Well, this chapter discusses proactive approaches to put anxiety behind you and, more importantly, ways to take your relationship with Jesus to a far higher level.

It takes time to train our minds and hearts to break the bondage we have to our evil habits. We must look into various ways we can unleash the powers of the Holy Spirit. People often talk in our society about desiring to be book smart and street smart. My friends often joked that I wasn't always at the top of my game when it came to street smarts. I think that's OK. While being book smart and street smart is fine, everyone would really be blessed if we strived to be as spiritually smart as possible. Being spiritually smart is what will save our souls when judgement day unexpectedly hits us.

The Power of Prayer

One approach is through praying. Praying is the ultimate link to connecting with the Lord. It is a time for us to have an intimate moment with our heavenly Father. We need to speak to God *and* listen intently to him. I must confess that listening has never been my forte. Just ask my wife and friends, and they will agree. With my anxiety came racing thoughts, so I couldn't focus and wasn't able to make sense of things. When I prayed, I would often repeat the same words, begging to be healed. I was lost in misery.

As I have grown closer to Jesus, I've sensed numerous things I could do better to grow this relationship. The first thing has been about finding someplace very quiet where I could focus. Without this calm environment, I don't believe my prayers could be effective and answered. Another thing about prayer is that it should be conversational and meaningful. Don't hold back from the Lord, because he knows your thoughts and needs. There's no reason to be shy and ashamed, because you are loved more than you will ever imagine as a child of God.

Making Prayer a Priority

It's always been difficult to make praying my number one priority. They used to tell us in Bible camp to pray first thing in the morning instead of waiting until the end of the day when we go to bed. They said to pray to God first thing in the morning so he can make an impact on the rest of our day. If we wait until almost bedtime, the day is done, and we're tired and can't give Jesus full energy and focus. The Lord is not an afterthought. Let's not treat him that way.

How to Pray

While praying, we can focus on several areas. First of all, we must give thanks to the Lord. Our Creator deserves the highest praise, and it's important we show our gratitude. If this is a new thing for you, it can be very helpful to make a list of people you treasure, your notable accomplishments, ways you have grown personally, storms you have survived, among other things. In addition, sometimes it's easy to forget the basic survival things we all need: food, shelter, and safety. The list is truly endless because every good thing is from above, coming from the Father.

After gratitude, we must humble ourselves with repentance and confession. No one is perfect, and we shouldn't expect to be, but we can *strive* to be perfect since it's a process. Part of that process is admitting when we've fallen short of the glory of God like everyone else and how we can have God help us grow spiritually. In 2 Chronicles 7:14, the Lord said, "If my people, who are called by my name, will humble themselves and pray and seek my face and turn from their wicked ways, then I will hear from heaven, and I will forgive their sin and will heal their land."

Biblical Lesson: This verse should be a daily reminder that we use to grow our relationship with the Lord and cease our sinful ways. There's no doubt we all make mistakes often, but we need to count on relying on God to get better. It starts with us repenting, and then listening to Jesus for guidance.

Once we have repented, then we can end our prayer by asking for blessings. We should not be hesitant about asking our Savior for things. It begins by asking for guidance, especially when we are trying to grow from our weaknesses. In addition, we can ask for individual requests from the Lord where only he can bless us. Scripture states in 1 John 5:14, "This is the confidence we have in approaching God: that if we ask anything according to his will, he hears us."

Biblical Lesson: The key thing is that we should keep our requests aligned with God's will.

The Power of Fasting

I admit that, until recently, I had limited knowledge about what fasting entailed since I had never tried it. At the time of this writing, I've fasted twice. The first one was not eating or drinking *anything* except water for two days. The purpose of the fast was not diet-related. The point was to use it as a spiritual tool to draw closer to the Lord. When your mind and body are demanding food, you should direct your attention to the Lord because your flesh is reminding you how delicious a juicy burger tastes, but this is just a temporary inconvenience that cannot even compare to the greatness of your God.

Many times people use this prayer and reflection time during fasting to get insight from Jesus on how to handle certain situations. Shortly after I did the two-day fast, I felt guidance towards a gentle mindset. Going forward, I felt better equipped to handle the devil's schemes. Also, I went through a fourteen-day fast from social media and surfing the web on sports websites. It was incredibly hard. With technology growing and making life more convenient, this craving for instant gratification only continues to expand as the digital age transforms.

Whenever I felt like giving up, there was Scripture that helped in Luke 4:1–4, "Jesus, full of the Holy Spirit, left the Jordan and was led by the Spirit into the wilderness, where for forty days he was tempted by the devil. He ate nothing during those days, and at the end of them, he was hungry. The devil said to him, 'If you are the Son of God, tell this stone to become bread.' Jesus answered, 'It is written: Man shall not live on bread alone.'"

Biblical Lesson: Even Jesus was tempted and mocked by the devil when fasting, but he didn't give in to the pressure. Jesus said we should only follow God's Word and not fall for tricks by the devil. Instead, we need to plug in and draw closer to the Lord.

The Power of Giving

This can be done with talents, time, and wealth. When it comes to giving, I have room for growth. Sometimes I struggle to consistently give. Sometimes I have given money to a homeless person on the street or paid for a stranger's meal.

I'm trying to give to others while taking steps to grow my heart. The bottom line is that I need to give more consistently.

When it comes to growing our hearts, there is an eye-opening passage in Mark 12:41–44:

> "Jesus sat down opposite the place where the offerings were put and watched the crowd putting their money into the temple treasury. Many rich people threw in large amounts. But a poor widow came and put in two very small copper coins, worth only a few cents. Calling his disciples to him, Jesus said, 'Truly I tell you, this poor widow has put more into the treasury than all the others. They all gave out of their wealth; but she, out of her poverty, put in everything—all she had to live on.'"

This is where I struggle, and this is the type of Scripture most of us need.

Biblical Lesson: This verse is an eye-opener because it shows what God's children are capable of giving. There is so much potential for everyone to do so much more. What are we willing to sacrifice for Jesus who gave everything dying for our sins?

We all have an area in our lives where we need a miracle from the Lord. We can grow spiritually when we give of ourselves, and we are a gift from God made in his image. Our body is his body, and we were all given very different talents in differing degrees. Regardless of our talent level,

Jesus knows we can all love on others. Scripture says in 1 Corinthians 12:4–6, "There are different kinds of gifts, but the same Spirit distributes them. There are different kinds of service, but the same Lord. There are different kinds of working, but in all of them and in everyone it is the same God at work." Remember, you are always able to help others.

Biblical Lesson: The Lord created all of his children with unique gifts because there are so many different needs. Jesus wants the world to have a diversity of talent available. No one should question their spiritual gifts.

Time is another way we can spread the word of God. We can do acts of charity by being nice to each other, helping out a neighbor needing assistance, and going out of our way for acts of service. Yet our time is short on this planet. In Romans 13:11, the Lord said, "And do this, understanding the present time: The hour has already come for you to wake up from your slumber, because our salvation is nearer now when we first believed."

Biblical Lesson: The word *already* in this passage is so remarkable because we have no excuse but to set aside our qualms and begin serving God now. Now. Now.

I'm attempting in every thought and action to separate myself further from the devil and bring myself closer to the light with God. This requires learning the endless wisdom that comes from knowing Jesus and building a relationship with him. I have a long journey ahead, as many do, but I know that I am miles ahead of where I was years ago. I pray the same for you. It's a never-ending quest to learn how to be spiritually smart from Jesus Christ.

Remember: In every thought, decision, and action, reflect on how you can use God's love to make a difference. Seek clarity from the Lord on your special gifts and how you can use them to help others.

Take Action: Stop being shy and hesitant about your faith. Shine your light in every way possible through giving, fasting, and praying. Influence as many friends, family, and strangers as possible to learn more about the truth of God today.

ABOUT THE AUTHOR

As a kid, Zach Ribble wrote hundreds of pages of stories but never finished any book he started. Over twenty years later, after suffering with debilitating anxiety that brought him closer to God, he felt motivated to finish his first book so he could help others break the chains.

He has worked as a journalist and a public relations specialist and has won numerous awards as a human resource specialist for his ability to help others find jobs that fit their personality and strengths.

When he isn't working, he is passionate about growing in Christ, bringing others closer to the Lord, and engaging in his hobbies. Besides writing, Zach enjoys football, basketball, board games, and spending time with his family. He lives with his wife, Jennifer, and two girls, Alexis and Zoe, in Michigan. He hopes his readers will learn there is always hope and peace in Jesus Christ.

CAN YOU HELP?

Thank You For Reading My Book!

I really appreciate all your feedback, and I love hearing what you have to say.

I need your input to make the next version of this book and my future books better.

Please leave me an honest review on Amazon, letting me know what you thought of the book.

Thanks so much!

Zach Ribble